A New Beginning

SUNY Series in Speech Communication
Dudley D. Cahn, Editor

A New Beginning

A Textual Frame Analysis of
the Political Campaign Film

Joanne Morreale

State University of New York Press

Published by
State University of New York Press, Albany

© 1991 State University of New York

Printed in the United States of America

For information, address State University of New York
Press, State University Plaza, Albany, N.Y., 12246

Production by E. Moore
Marketing by Theresa A. Swierzowski

Library of Congress Cataloging-in-Publication Data

Morreale, Joanne, 1956-
    A new beginning : a textual frame analysis of the political
campaign film / Joanne Morreale.
        p.   cm. — (SUNY series in speech communication)
    Includes bibliographical references (p.   ) and index.
    ISBN 0-7914-0608-3 (alk. paper). — ISBN 0-7914-0609-1 (pbk. :
alk. paper)
    1. Republican Party (U.S. : 1854)—Public relations.
    2. Advertising, Political—United States. 3. Television in
politics—United States. 4. Presidents—United States-
-Election—1984. 5. Reagan, Ronald. I. Title. II. Series.
    JK2357 1984a
    324.2784—dc20   90-9904
                                                                  CIP

10 9 8 7 6 5 4 3 2 1

Contents

Acknowledgments

I would like to thank the many people who have made this work possible. A number of friends and colleagues contributed their valuable time and insights. I am especially grateful to Lee Cahn, who helped me refine and develop my ideas, and who provided immeasurable advice and encouragement. I also appreciate the contribution of Priscilla Ross at SUNY Press, who expeditiously handled the production process and made helpful suggestions throughout.

I would like to mention Herb Simons of Temple University, who advised and guided me during the initial stages of this project. Tim Corrigan, Paul Swann, and Ralph Towne also offered me their expertise. Stephanie Stewart and Melanie Rae Thon provided editorial assistance and valuable criticism. Thanks go to all of them, and to the others who have read and commented upon earlier versions of this work.

Thanks also go to my students and colleagues at Northeastern University for their lively discussions of *A New Beginning*, and to my parents for making it possible for me to pursue my interests in the first place. Finally, my deepest appreciation goes to Richard Lewis, who provided assistance and support throughout this project.

Introduction

On August 23, 1984, as the Republican National Convention was approaching its finale, conventioneers were already assured that Ronald Reagan would be their candidate for the November presidential elections. The convention itself lacked suspense. Greater interest was generated by A New Beginning, the Republicans' half-million-dollar celebration of the first four years of Ronald Reagan's presidency. The film, narrated by Ronald Reagan, consisted of a series of short vignettes drawn from news events, interviews, images of America and its citizens, a music video, a Reagan "home movie," and excerpts from speeches. This unusual combination of images was intercut to convey the Republican campaign message of renewed hope, optimism, and patriotism across the United States.

Ronald Reagan won the 1984 election by the largest margin of electoral votes in American presidential history. He was one of the most popular presidents in modern times, the "Great Communicator" who consistently received high personal approval ratings even among those who disagreed with his policies. His appeal was largely dependent on two interrelated factors: his use of rhetoric which resonated with the needs and desires of the American people; and his ability to use the electronic media.

Throughout his eight years in office, Reagan and his aides played to television's strengths and weaknesses. Television is an aural and visual medium; therefore, they coordinated words and images to convey coherent messages. An increasingly large number of Americans rely solely on television for their news; hence, the White House strategically released positive pictures in time to make the evening news. Throughout the 1984 campaign, the Republicans repeatedly used television to express a simple theme: America is back on top, thanks to Ronald Reagan.

The Republicans underscored their commitment to televisual

communication in *A New Beginning,* the eighteen-minute political campaign film that was initially presented at the Dallas convention. The Republicans characterized it as a "documentary" and a "news event" that would be used to introduce Ronald Reagan at the Republican National Convention. Their decision to use the film instead of a speech was an obvious attempt to ensure network coverage of the $425,000 project.[1] The networks had aired political campaign films at conventions since 1952, but in 1984 they decided to truncate their convention coverage, which meant that they would not necessarily broadcast the Republican film. However, the networks had already carried Ted Kennedy's nominating speech for candidate Walter Mondale at the Democratic convention, so the Republicans argued that their "nominating speech"—albeit a film—should also be shown.

The three major networks were reluctant to accede to the Republican ploy. Their hesitation was fueled in part by a public protest letter from Charles Manatt, chairman of the Democratic National Committee. He complained that as the networks had not broadcast Walter Mondale's campaign film because they considered it to be a commercial, the Reagan film should not be shown.

The networks needed to decide whether Manatt was right, or whether the film was an acceptable alternative to the nominating speech. If they considered it to be a documentary or a news event, they ought to air it as part of their convention coverage; if it was primarily an unpaid advertisement for Ronald Reagan, they would have grounds not to show the film. Edward M. Joyce, president of CBS News who decided not to air the film, expressed his opinion: "It represents the dividing line between advertising and journalism. It is a very skillfully done commercial and deserves great respect for that. But it did not represent the best use of eighteen minutes of our television news coverage. . . . A live speech has journalistic merit."[2] Reuven Frank, executive producer of NBC news, was even more disparaging, "I hate the film. It's demeaning, an obvious attempt to manipulate the public."[3] Yet NBC opted to air *A New Beginning* in its entirety, announcing that public interest, generated by the controversy over the film, had made it a news event. CNN, the cable news network, also broadcast it, while ABC and CBS showed excerpts only.

The characteristics of *A New Beginning* that made the networks uneasy are exactly those that make it worthy of critical attention. The best of its kind, the televised film may have transformed the art of political filmmaking. It was designed for a television audience and structured as a hybrid generic form: part advertisement and part documentary. Much of the film consisted of the carefully crafted, elaborately staged scenes characteristic of advertisements. Some of its images were taken directly from the "It's Morning in America" advertising campaign run during the 1984 presidential primaries. Settings recognizable from feel-good beer advertisements echoed those of product advertisements running at the time; the film also incorporated a music video of the then-popular country-and-western song "God Bless the USA" by singer Lee Greenwood. On the other hand, the elements of *A New Beginning* typically associated with documentary film production were archival and news footage, travelogue footage of foreign places, voice-over narration, still photographs, "expert" testimonials, and interviews with ordinary Americans.

The film was a mixed-genre documentary and advertisement; a survey taken by *Adweek* immediately after the Republican National Convention found that respondents confused paid advertising and unpaid media coverage of political events. Further, Reagan seemed to be benefiting from these misconceptions.[4] The film slipped easily into whatever genre was most expedient.

A New Beginning marked the coming-of-age of the televisual political campaign film. While many presidential candidates have had a biographical film that conveyed their campaign themes and issues, *A New Beginning* established the televisual political campaign film as a centerpiece of the presidential election campaign. By the next presidential election, candidates George Bush and Michael Dukakis both had films, aired on national television, that preceded their acceptance addresses at their respective conventions. In four short years, that which had been so controversial was accepted without comment by the networks and the press.

A New Beginning, as an exemplar of the contemporary televisual political campaign film, also demonstrated the sophisticated use of visual communication in presidential politics. The film served as a display, indeed the quintessential display, of Ronald Reagan's rhetoric: discourse characterized by optimistic, upbeat, patriotic themes that emphasized a renewed sense of national identity and unity. Its producers acknowledged that it was their fullest and most coherent presentation of Ronald Reagan and his rhetorical appeals.

The film was produced by the "Tuesday Team," an ad hoc group of advertising experts assembled to assist with the campaign, and written by Phil Dusenberry, executive creative director of the

BBD&O advertising agency and originator of the "Pepsi Generation" campaign. The Tuesday Team's use of modern marketing techniques enabled Reagan to reaffirm traditional America in *A New Beginning*. The team relied extensively upon population polls, surveys, demographic data, and market pre-testing strategies, as well as the already established visual symbolism of advertising. They were allocated close to $25 million—more than one-half of the entire campaign budget—in order to create innovative, high production-value political advertisements.[5]

The increasingly prevalent use of televisual advertising techniques by presidential candidates has been documented in books such as Joe McGinnis's *The Selling of the President 1968*, Kathleen Jamieson's *Packaging the Presidency: A History and Criticism of Presidential Campaign Advertising*, Edwin Diamond and Stephen Bates' *The Spot: The Rise of Political Advertising of Television*, and Daniel Boorstin's *The Image: A Guide to Pseudo-Events in America*. This book extends their work by conducting an in-depth analysis of a single film to assess both the conditions and ramifications of the predominance of the image over the word in American presidential politics.

Both *Packaging the Presidency* and *The Spot* discuss the ways that politicians have used television and modes of communication specific to it to "sell" themselves. Since Franklin Roosevelt first made effective use of radio to address the American people en masse (a practice carried on by Ronald Reagan), politicians have become increasingly aware of the potential of the mass media to help gain the support of the voting public. It was not until the late 1950s that television and television advertising began to be used extensively in political campaigns; the 1960 Kennedy-Nixon television debates focused public and political attention on the need for candidates to project a positive image on television. It was widely claimed that Nixon lost the debates because he did not convey a wholesome image. His subsequent campaign in 1968, documented in Joe McGinnis's *The Selling of the President*, was almost exclusively a media campaign.

Moreover, as Boorstin first noted in *The Image*, the broadcast media have increasingly been used to produce or create rather than to simply represent events. Politicians, in particular, have learned to orchestrate events that do not exist other than for the television cameras; the spectacle of reality is the reality. Jean Baudrillard, in *Simulations*, goes one step further than Boorstin and asserts that contemporary culture is characterized by simulations, images of the real that have no referents. Images become the reality they ostensibly represent.

The Reagan administration broke new ground through its deft manufacture of pseudoevents, passed off as "photo opportunities." *A New Beginning* incorporated many of these artificial constructions: Reagan riding on horseback through the lush hillsides of his California ranch; Ronald and Nancy Reagan walking among the gravestones of American servicemen who died in the Normandy landings; Reagan cheerfully sharing a cafeteria lunch with American troops on the front line of the Korean DMZ (demilitarized zone). Even the controversy over whether or not to air *A New Beginning* transformed the film into a pseudoevent. In a deeper way, the entire film was a simulation whose fantasy of a revitalized America appeared to be reality for many Americans.

The sophisticated rhetorical use of images to simulate reality distinguished the Reagan campaign from its predecessors. Even though the Republicans used the film as a substitute for a speech, it communicated far more powerfully through visual images than it did through words. I have already noted that the Reagan White House showed a keen awareness of television as a visual communication form. In an interview before the election, Reagan's Chief of Staff Michael Deaver stressed this point: "Television changes everything so much. . . . The image becomes all important. . . . Visuals become necessary to get something across."[6] Deaver also remarked, "Television elects presidents."[7] Each scene of *A New Beginning* demonstrated a simple yet profoundly held belief of the Reagan White House and the Tuesday Team: American culture is more visually than verbally oriented. *A New Beginning* was a product of a culture devoted to images.

My method of televisual rhetorical criticism, which I refer to as textual frame analysis, makes use of insights drawn from contemporary film criticism, television criticism, political and cultural studies. I wish to provide theoretical insight into the way that *A New Beginning* constructed a picture of the world, the way it made that world intelligible, and the way that it worked ideologically, that is, how it masked its own work of construction. My task as a rhetorical critic is to increase understanding of how its meanings were made, how they were presented and represented, and how these meanings related to their cultural milieu.

More specifically, a rhetorical analysis of *A New Beginning* accounts for its apparent success and creates a clearer understanding of the contemporary televisual political campaign film. I will show how the Republicans used the film to present their vision of resurgent hope and optimism as reality, how the film helped them to orient the political majority to Republican thinking, and most importantly, how a communicative form such as *A New Beginning* contributed to Ronald Reagan's landslide election victory in 1984.

I begin my study by contextualizing *A New Beginning* with a brief exposition of its historical antecedents; I also describe its influence on the 1988 presidential campaign. Tracing the development of the genre demonstrates the increasing importance of the televisual political campaign film; similarly, the Reagan film's impact on George Bush's 1988 campaign suggests that the genre continues to evolve as a televisual form.

Textual frame analysis then begins with an explication of the framing of *A New Beginning*, understood as the way that the viewing experience was organized to convey a particular definition of reality. Frames determine the way that experiences are defined as being of one type, or order, rather than another. By confusing genres, levels, and spaces of televisual discourse typically regarded to be distinct, the Republicans more easily simulated reality.

Next, I discuss ideology as the particular frame, or definition of reality, that the Republicans wanted to convey. I provide a brief, necessarily selective, account of Reagan's political credo. This provides background for understanding the conservative frame, or ideology, constructed by the film.

A close examination of the text itself reveals the Republicans' use of rebirth rhetoric to communicate their ideological positions to the American public. The film is structured as a rhetorical myth; myths are ideologies in that they work to create a unified and coherent reality, and to reinforce the notion that a particular set of beliefs, values, and attitudes are right and true. The Republicans used rebirth rhetoric as a way of framing "reality." The film was structured as a mythic rebirth ritual, while its content indicated the rebirth of American myths.

Particular myths were communicated by a poetic assemblage of stock images, referred to as visual clichés, that resonated with the needs and desires of the American people. Artfully deployed clichés were specifically televisual means of communication that differentiated *A New Beginning* from other forms of political discourse. Clichés are not only preeminent in a culture increasingly oriented toward the visual; used strategically, they can be powerful persuasive tools.

Textual frame analysis, in brief, moves from an examination of framing, to ideology, to myths that express ideologies, to the particular ways that myths are communicated. The method includes evaluation, which in this case entails a criticism of Reagan's communication strategies with regard to *A New Beginning*.

This book ends with a chapter on method, where I provide a more detailed exposition of textual frame analysis and place it within the context of other critical methods. I demonstrate the utility and necessity for televisual rhetorical criticism to comment upon, and thus re-frame, contemporary political discourse.

1 Political Campaign Films

Boy, is that a powerful documentary . . . is that really me?
—Ronald Reagan[1]

The Republicans spent nearly $500,000 on *A New Beginning* in 1984, in contrast to the $77,000 the Democrats spent in entirety for television advertising in 1952.[2] The videotaped film was a cornerstone of the campaign, and as such was put to many uses. Parts of the "documentary" were used as spot commercials during the primary and general election campaigns. It preceded the acceptance address that marked President Reagan's first "live" appearance at the convention, thus assuring network coverage and a large viewing audience. In fact, twenty-three million people were tuned in to the convention.[3] Later, the film was combined with footage from the convention and parts of the acceptance address, and rebroadcast as a paid thirty-minute commercial. The commercial aired simultaneously on all three entertainment networks and cable networks WTBS, CBN, and ESPN; thirty million people saw this version.[4] *A New Beginning* was later recut with up-to-date images and rebroadcast at the 1988 Republican National Convention, and George Bush used sequences from it in his own 1988 political campaign film. (Bush, too, used his political campaign film immediately prior to the acceptance speech at the convention). These multiple functions helped the Republicans keep their messages simple and consistent across two presidencies; even more pragmatically, the campaigns reaped the returns from their investments.

A New Beginning initially gained notoriety as an admixture of news event, documentary, and political advertisement. It was also the latest incarnation of the genre of political campaign films, which has existed in some form since 1952, when television first became an essential tool in national politics. Both Eisenhower and Stevenson aired thirty-minute films in 1952. Eisenhower's election-eve broadcast combined live and filmed footage. His spot series, *Eisenhower Answers America* consisted of ordinary Americans asking questions that were edited together with the candidate's answers: an early manipulation of frames where discrete events became unified as one continuous television "event." This technique was further refined in 1956 when Eisenhower appeared on a split-screen alongside the people who questioned him, even though his answers were prerecorded. The Republicans also made extensive use of the five-minute spot commercial in 1956, while the Democrats initiated "televised production spots"—advertisements which did not depict the candidate.[5]

Though Eisenhower's, and to some extent Stevenson's, media strategies prefigured the political campaign film, John F. Kennedy's thirty-minute "biography," *The New Frontier*, became emblematic of the genre.[6] The film combined documentary techniques with still photographs to produce a chronological record of Kennedy's personal history, featuring his school career, service to his country, dedication to family values, and qualifications for public office. He was shown to be a leader (although later candidates were sometimes presented as men of the people, depending on situational exigencies and strategies). The film stressed Kennedy's experience as a war hero and a senator from Massachusetts; he met with military and foreign leaders, and he concluded the film by averring his commitment to peace.

Its themes set the tone for later films: Kennedy promised to improve the economy, to keep America strong militarily, and to maintain peace. In this case, some of the negative issues that plagued the Kennedy campaign were explicitly addressed. He spoke to disgruntled coal miners in Virginia; he also responded to a question about whether his Catholicism would interfere with his ability to govern. Kennedy assured the questioner, and thus the viewer, that it would not.

Structurally, *The New Frontier* simulated newsreel footage, complete with stark black-and-white images, the anonymous voice of a narrator, and a static camera. One of *The New Frontier's* innovations was the use of on-location shooting to film Kennedy as he delivered speeches. There were no close-ups, nor did he appear "live" on camera to address the audience directly at any time. Rather, he was filmed in cinema-verité style, as if he were oblivious to the presence of the camera. The only indication of the media's presence was a microphone that Kennedy held in his hand as he spoke amidst crowds of people.

The film did not use many techniques of implication and association to make its points, nor did it incorporate the aesthetic qualities of advertisements. Clips of Kennedy's oratory on the campaign trail reiterated his catchphrase, America as the "New Frontier," and illustrated his vision of a prosperous, militarily strong, and peaceful America.

After 1960, as politicians increasingly made use of media techniques based upon advertising, political campaign films became correspondingly more sophisticated. The aberrant *Choice*, produced for Barry Goldwater without his approval by the Citizens for Goldwater/Mothers for Moral America group, deserves mention for its strong use of implication and innuendo as argumentative forms. Images of moral turpitude in Johnson's America were intercut with wholesome, idyllic images of Goldwater's America, offering viewers a "choice" between the two versions. NBC agreed to air the film; although the network demanded that an image of a woman in a topless bathing suit be cut, racist images of blacks were deemed permissible. Goldwater himself ordered the inflammatory film withdrawn prior to its airing.[7] Yet the visual techniques of implication and innuendo carried on.

As political campaign directors have become more media-savvy, the films have increasingly combined techniques common to documentaries, advertising, and news. Initially, political campaign films were aired on national television as part of the networks' convention coverage, or they were paid for as advertising for the general campaign. Often, they aired during the convention and again during the closing weeks of the campaign. In 1972, Nixon's *Portrait of a President* was shown at the Republican National Convention, while *The Nixon Years: Change Without Chaos* (which incorporated footage from the first film) was later broadcast as a paid political film. (This recalls how *A New Beginning* was first aired at the convention, then a half-hour version played on national television to initiate the general campaign.) Many of the same personnel who made up Nixon's team of advertising experts, called the November Group, became Reagan's Tuesday Team in 1984; thus Reagan's campaign film repeated a strategy that worked for Nixon: replaying images that highlighted the strengths of the candidate.

Probably the film that most sharply contrasts with the Reagan film, while still showing the development of the genre, is *The Democratic Faith: The Johnson Years* (1968). Like other campaign films, it moved from a presentation of the man, to his domestic accomplishments, to foreign affairs. Johnson visited the military troops, although he did not promote identification by dressing in uniform as Reagan later did. He appeared at a summit with foreign leaders, just as Reagan portrayed his meeting with the Chinese premier. Finally, the Johnson film ended with a final affirmation of his commitment to peace.

After Johnson announced on the eve of the primary that he would not run for reelection, the film was used to summarize the legacy of the Democratic Party, with a focus on Lyndon Johnson's term in office. If Johnson had decided to seek a second term, this film would have been used exclusively for his campaign. After its initial use at the Democratic convention, it was shown on NBC as a half-hour political "special."

The Johnson Years, produced eight years after *The New Frontier*, indicates the genre's evolving admixture of documentary and advertising styles. The film opens with Johnson, wearing a cowboy hat, standing by a river as he reflects upon the course of the country since the New Deal. Sentimental music plays; then this quiet moment is interrupted by newsreel footage of every Democratic president since Roosevelt. Powerful, emotional footage of Kennedy's funeral follows, with close-ups of burning candles and people in mourning. Johnson provides the voice-over narration, although his commentary is not "live," nor does it pertain to the images. His remarks are taken from earlier speeches. Unlike the Kennedy film, which merely depicts the candidate as he delivers speeches, the Johnson film matches the candidate's words with emotional images.

Further, Johnson does not narrate the entire film. Gregory Peck serves this function, illustrating a move toward famous, recognizable voices that speak for the candidate. In 1976, for instance, Joe Garagiola speaks for Gerald Ford, as E. G. Marshall does for Jimmy Carter. Ex-movie star and professional narrator Ronald Reagan speaks for himself in the 1984 film.

The Johnson film differed from *A New Beginning* in content as well as structure. *The Johnson Years* testified to the Democrats' commitment to the principles of the New Deal, a program that Reagan aimed to dismantle. Johnson and the Democrats were lauded for achievements of little importance to Ronald Reagan. Civil rights, affirmative action, Medicaid, Headstart, education, and Johnson's "War on Poverty" were central issues in the earlier film. Indigent families in Appalachia and urban ghettoes existed in this issue-oriented film. Foreign policy and the war in Vietnam were discussed even though these topics were detrimental to the Democrats in 1968.

Following the Johnson film, the campaign films used by Gerald Ford and Jimmy Carter in 1976 illustrated the increasingly sophisticated media techniques of the genre. In both cases, images were highly stylized although both remained rooted in the documentary mode of exposition. Ford's film, for example, opened with former baseball player Joe Garagiola seated in Air Force One. He introduced the film, telling the viewers the theme (Ford's candidacy) and how it would be developed. He began, "We'll see a documentary about his background, job, family, hopes for America . . . and then we'll hear from Gerald Ford himself."

The film developed chronologically, although the "documentary" footage of Ford as an athlete, scholar, military man, family man and public figure was intercut with interviews of "authoritative" figures. Singer Pearl Bailey voiced her support for Ford as part of Garagiola's introduction; later, members of Ford's college football team, friends from Yale, and members of Congress and the Senate testified to his character and leadership skills.

Unlike Carter, Ford primarily needed to establish his authority in 1976. His appeal was not populist; he did not rely upon the voices of ordinary people on the street to lend credibility to his candidacy. *A New Beginning*, on the other hand, illustrated Reagan's ability to reconcile these two opposing requirements; he managed to present himself as a leader and a man of the people in a seemingly noncontradictory manner.

The Ford film did, however, make use of strategies similar to those that structured the Reagan film. Visual clichés abounded: Air Force One, the American flag, the Statue of Liberty, productive farms, lush harvests, construction workers, people streaming out of factories. Ford's message was strikingly similar to Ronald Reagan's in 1984: he promised to cut taxes, reduce inflation, decrease government bureaucracy, make the United States strong militarily, and be a man of peace. There was even an attempt made to portray an American rebirth with images of the Bicentennial celebrations. Ford's claim that Americans had endured a period of conflict was supported with images of discontented Americans gathered in large demonstrations (of what it was not clear, nor did Ford specify the hardships that Americans had experienced).

A New Beginning alluded to past discontent through a sequence of barely discernible newspaper and magazine headlines proclaiming high interest rates and rocketing inflation, followed by another that heralded the economic recovery. These reinforced the authenticity of

Reagan's claims for a new beginning, and mitigated the potentially dispiriting effect of such reminders.

The Ford film depicted vivid images of conflict not necessarily located in the past. The Reagan film portrayed a revitalized America; the Ford film merely hinted at the possibility. The Ford film concluded with a song, "I'm Feeling Good About America," and a vignette of positive, upbeat images of America. But 1976 was too soon after Watergate for a Republican president to be leading a spiritual revival. The candidate's themes, aims, and objectives were similar to those of Ronald Reagan in 1984. Unlike Reagan, however, Ford could not associate himself with American resurgence.

The Ford film was not so highly produced as *A New Beginning*, but then neither was the candidate. Ford was not a central figure who rendered all of the images coherent. Further, Ford was hardly adept at televisual communication. In his one attempt to directly address the television audience at the end of the film, he did not use a teleprompter, and was obviously reading his speech rather than "conversing." He was filmed in a medium shot as a static "talking head," and there were no extreme close-ups that would have conveyed a feeling of intimacy with the viewer.

The visual techniques that structured the Ford film were not unified, and the images failed to convey the authority and authenticity of the candidate. Singer Pearl Bailey, for example, voiced her support for Ford by proclaiming, "Lord knows he's made mistakes . . . but he is trying."

In the opposing camp, Carter's 1976 campaign film *Jimmy Who?* also shared televisual characteristics with *A New Beginning*. It, too, included a song and had a musical score. It was not issue-oriented; interviews were conducted with people on the street who made comments such as, "I think he's sexy," and "What's wrong with a peanut farmer?" The film was in tune with the times, as it emphasized Carter's status as a Washington outsider and a (millionaire) man of the people.

The Carter film was lighthearted, using visual techniques such as animation and split-screen video. It was fast-paced and primarily a visual communication form. In one sequence, a montage of political cartoons of Carter, with his exaggerated grin, appeared on screen. The situational constraints surrounding both *Jimmy Who?* and *A New Beginning* suggested that neither needed to be issue-oriented. In the wake of Watergate, Carter needed to stress his integrity rather than his command of political issues; in the aftermath of Carter's dismal four years and Reagan's apparently successful first term in office, the 1984 election was virtually no contest.

In 1980, the Reagan campaign produced an eight-minute film that tentatively established the theme of a new beginning. Carter, on the other hand, stopped smiling. His thirty-minute film in 1980 was less innovative and visual than the 1976 film. It was issue-oriented and filmed in the traditional campaign documentary style. Preoccupied with reestablishing his credibility, Carter reverted to familiar forms. The film stressed his leadership qualities and experience on the job. One principal disadvantage was that it was too forthcoming; it also referred to his weaknesses and the problems that remained unresolved.

A New Beginning, like the Reagan 1984 campaign in general, emphasized only the positive. Though the Reagan administration was indeed subject to criticism, this was not made apparent. The Republican film had the theme that America was experiencing an economic and spiritual rebirth. Its visual and structural devices, notably the presentation of the president himself as narrator, all worked to strengthen and reinforce this vision.

The Mondale film, on the other hand, emphasized that there were problems. In striking contrast to *A New Beginning*, the candidate was presented as mortal rather than divine. "What was your nickname in high school?" an off-camera voice asks Walter Mondale. "Crazy legs," he replies, with a self-deprecatory grin. The Mondale film had no song or slick visual techniques. Like its competitor, it incorporated many visual clichés that symbolize America. These were highlighted when CBS reporter Jeff Greenfield compared and contrasted the two films on the evening of the Republican National Convention (in lieu of showing the Reagan film). Similar images from both films were juxtaposed upon a split-screen video, thus emphasizing their differences. For example, while both films included images of the Statue of Liberty, the Mondale footage showed the statue before its massive reconstruction project had begun. The footage was old and outdated; the images presented a static figure to the viewer. In *A New Beginning*, however, a dynamic camera zoomed in on the statue, which was being repaired. It, like America, was being "rebuilt." Even this simple cliché conveyed the message of the film. More important, the Reagan film celebrated present-day reality, while the Mondale film was a negative reminder of the past.

All indications point to the continuing development and entrenchment of political campaign films. In 1984, *A New Beginning* assumed a prominent position as part of the reelection campaign. It served as a microcosm of the tone, themes, and strategies of the 1984 campaign. It offered a substitute for a speech; it provided a condensed version of the aims and accomplishments of the Reagan administration; finally, it encompassed the best of the advertising strategies and the media-management skills of the Reagan advisers.

Such an accomplishment was not lost on George Bush or Michael Dukakis in 1988. Both candidates had campaign films, which they aired prior to their acceptance speeches at their conventions, as spot advertisements, and as parts of election-eve specials. The Dukakis film featured his cousin, the actress Olympia Dukakis, as narrator who literally walked viewers through the otherwise unremarkable film. Bush, who used many of the same media managers as Reagan, learned Reagan's lessons well, both in terms of general campaign strategy and the campaign film in particular. The Bush film extended Reagan's principally by mimicking its techniques. It used the same campaign song and images of Americans building, making, doing; it was structured as a nonsequential series of short vignettes that made use of modes of presentation characteristic of news and documentary genres. Interviews with "talking heads" were filmed in medium- to close-shot as they addressed the camera, while Ronald Reagan acted as an "eyewitness" who attested to the character of candidate Bush. Still photographs of the Bush family trekking West in the forties gave the film a documentary feel, although a filmed shot of the car traveling across the desert had to be a fabrication. An explication of the opening scene of the Bush film will show the accord between the two in more detail.

Like *A New Beginning*, the Bush film opens with a headline on a blank screen, "August 1988," ostensibly to locate the viewer in present time. This initial gambit is followed by a timeless slow-motion image of a young girl running through a grassy field. Her soft-focus image, accompanied by sentimental music, is reminiscent of an advertisement; quickly, this gentle image dissolves to white and is replaced by another headline that locates the viewer in the distant past: December 1941. Stark black-and-white images are complemented with harsh, throbbing music. Dissolve to white, and an anonymous narrator explains that America has faced many challenges throughout the century, and has found many people to meet those challenges. The unstated implication is that George Bush is one of them. The narrator's voice is accompanied by more black-and-white images of soldiers leaving for war that dissolve into them kissing

women goodbye. Rather than addressing the present and its challenges, the viewers are nostalgically returned to the site of one of
America's great victories. Graphics and black-and-white footage
serve as illustrative "proof" of the events to which the narrator
alludes; along with his anonymous voice of truth narration, they cue
the viewer to the film's authenticity.

Authenticity is also signaled by the use of still photographs in
lieu of moving images. Bush's own voice follows that of the narrator,
as Bush explains that he joined the army at eighteen because he wanted to become a pilot. Two still images accompany his words: one of
George with his young wife Barbara, and the second of Bush wearing
a pilot's cap and army uniform. These pictures, like the black-and-
white footage, corroborate his words. The offscreen narrator returns
to extol Bush's virtues as a war hero, describing the young army
pilot's exploits when he earned a distinguished flying cross on a
bombing run. His words, again, are illustrated by a black-and-white
image of planes and smoke.

Then, for the first time, there is a disjunctive cut in the film and
Bush's words and image are united in one shot. Color footage also
indicates a shift to the present as Bush, seated comfortably in the
White House, retells the experience that made him a hero. As he
speaks, his words are verified by documentary footage of World War
II. Pragmatically, this scene dispels charges of "wimpiness" that
plagued the candidate early on in his campaign. In addition, Bush's
mission fulfills the mythic pattern of the leader who is tested, overcomes challenge, and is the wiser for it.

Another dissolve transforms into the headlines on a movie marquee that advertise a newsreel titled "War Ends." The headlines nar-
rativize the film in a way that retains its implied authenticity. The
headlines show the passage of a significant moment; they also serve
as proof that it occurred. The movie image is itself reflexive: it may
unintentionally remind the viewer of the mediated nature of the
news then and now, and of the mediated nature of the Bush film
itself, that the viewer is, at that moment, watching a film about political "reality." While the 1984 Reagan campaign managers noted their
ability to manipulate the media, by 1988 the Bush team flaunted their
skills. (Later in the film, a montage of images shows Americans sitting in their living rooms watching television—another reflexive,
contemporary visual cliché.)

The "War Ends" marquee is followed by still photographs of
sailors returning home and people hugging. The music becomes soft

and sentimental; George Bush becomes part of the saga of American history, an important contributor to one of its most significant moments. Then cut back to the present with Bush seated in the White House. He articulates his desire to unify Americans, to make all a part of the same kind of team effort that resulted in victory in World War II. The scene finally ends with Barbara Bush who appears on camera to remind the viewers that her husband is, indeed, a caring man.

Not only does this opening scene implicitly set up Bush's alternating campaign strategy, advocating a nation that is kind and gentle, yet strong and prepared, it also articulates this message by blurring televisual genres. Overall, the preponderance of documentary images, intercut with more obviously mediated events constructed for the camera, disguise the fact that the film is, above all, an advertisement for George Bush. The advertisement is signaled by the young child in soft focus who appears at the very beginning (and later closes the film at its completion); yet this initial impression is overridden by the insistence of the documentary images to be perceived as representations of reality. The boundaries between different levels of mediation remain unclear, and different televisual genres are seamlessly linked through dissolves that blur distinctions. The film bolsters the candidate's credibility, and on an ideological level, creates a version of reality that appears to be natural and self-evidently true.

All of the political campaign films surveyed provide overviews of a particular candidate, summaries of who he was and what he stood for. *A New Beginning*, though, intensified the trend toward depicting a candidate, toward using images, symbols, and visual-communication conventions to create a positive climate surrounding the candidate. Most important, the film did not concede a separation between filmic and offscreen reality. In 1984, Ronald Reagan addressed viewers rather than readers, a strategy that worked for George Bush in 1988, and a strategy that will continue to elect presidents in the age of television.

2 Framing a Rebirth

*Ideology, in much recent cultural analysis, is understood in
Althusser's terms as "a system with its own logic and rigour"
of representations (images, myths, ideas or concepts, depending
on the case) endowed with a historical significance and role
within a given society. In other words, the work of masking,
unifying, or displacing contradictions goes on at one level in the
circulation of pre-formed ideas, common sense understandings,
the conventional wisdom of a given social group or society. On
another level, according to Althusser, this conventional wisdom
is materialized in the way we live our daily lives.*
                        —Christine Gledhill, "Klute 1"

A New Beginning offered Americans idealized
images of themselves and their president. By manipulating frames
(the communicative contexts that influence how particular messages
will be perceived) the Republicans provided an illusory sense of
national unity that was easily confused with reality. They managed
to create the impression of a homogenous country, populated by
prosperous and cheerful Americans who supported Ronald Reagan.
To begin to understand their success, let us explore frames in this
chapter and the way that they can be used to define a reality. Later
chapters each consider the film from a slightly altered frame, so that
the resultant prism of shifting yet related perspectives contributes
greater insight into the whole.

The Republicans made use of the codes and conventions of television to define a particular interpretive context for *A New Beginning*.
By manipulating frames, the boundaries that conventionally differentiate genres, levels, and even spaces of televisual discourse were rendered indistinguishable. As a result, the viewer was provided with
no position from which to differentiate fact from fiction, performance
from reality, or story from discourse. The voice and figure of Ronald

Reagan Reagan provided a point of orientation that unified all of the diverse sounds and images within the film. Reagan's dual role as narrator and character, both inside and outside of the film, helped to create a "fiction of discourse" with the viewing audience. What was actually a one-way transmission created the impression of a two-way dialogic relationship between Reagan and the viewer.

Framing

Erving Goffman has provided an extensive account of frames and how they are used to define and demarcate experience.[1] Frames are the organizational principles that govern interpretations of events; they are always determined by social convention. Frames, which may be implicit or explicit, facilitate communication by providing it with an order or structure within which events make sense. For example, both nonfiction and fiction are frames that govern viewers' expectations and help them to make sense of their experiences. As with all frames, certain experiences are both excluded and included, so that when one perceives a nonfiction, documentary frame, certain rules are believed to inhere: for example, shots are not manipulated, reality is captured in progress. Elaborate artifice, staged performance, or scenic orchestration are not typically perceived to be part of the documentary frame.

It is often the case that people are unable to define consciously the frames that demarcate their experience. Gregory Bateson has written that communication consists of three different levels of abstraction, or orders of experience that operate simultaneously.[2] The simplest level of first-order linguistic or denotative messages is where a word or image is equated with what it represents. For example, a televised image represents Ronald Reagan speaking at the D-Day ceremony. With second-order metalinguistic or connotative messages, the realm of rhetoric, the relationship between word or image and that to which it refers is arbitrary and more obviously determined by social convention. In this case, the event is coded as solemn, commemorative, formal in tone and atmosphere. Finally, third-level metacommunicative messages, or frames, provide tacit instructions for a receiver to interpret the first- and second-order messages included within them. Here the camera angles, shot compositions, and poor sound quality, as well as the viewer's knowledge of the historical actuality of the event, are messages that tell the viewer to interpret the event as nonfiction, as an unmediated representation of reality.

Metacommunicative frames distinguish different orders of experience. In particular, they enable communicants to discriminate between "factual" representation and fiction, or between denotative "reality" and simulation (i.e., play or fantasy, which both is and is not what it represents). Frames are therefore ideological in that they support one interpretive version of reality and necessarily exclude others. Invisibly, implicitly they order and organize perceptions. Thus, the reality of a given communication is constituted by interpretive frames that provide a delimited ground within which messages and events can be discerned.

Occluding Boundaries between Genres

The Republicans conveyed their vision of American resurgence in *A New Beginning* by omitting markers that would indicate different genres of televisual discourse, and thus would allow the viewer to establish different interpretive frames. The Republicans initially framed the film as a nonfiction news event at the Republican National Convention. This encouraged the television audience tuned into the event to perceive the film as a documentary, rather than an advertisement, or more bluntly, a propagandistic attempt to influence.

By framing the film as nonfiction, the Reagan campaign managers controlled the interpretive context in which it was to be viewed by determining the genre in which it was to be placed. Nonfiction films are believed to be more directly connected to reality than are advertisements. Although the Reagan film shared many characteristics with other highly mediated political campaign films, the Republicans created a set of viewer expectations that differed from those associated with fiction, advertisements, or other specifically political films. As nonfiction, the film gained credibility; it evoked responses more typical of less overtly mediated representations.

The admixture of visual forms and genres that constituted *A New Beginning* ranged from those understood to be highly mediated, and obviously marked by a rhetorical presence, to those perceived to be unmediated reflections of reality. These genres are characterized by Goffman's distinction of primary frameworks as either "social" or "natural."[3] Advertisements and fiction films are signs of social frameworks, which viewers know to be mediated products of human intention. News and documentary genres are signs of natural frameworks, where viewers believe events to be "caused" by reality rather than vested interests.

Fundamentally, both natural and social frameworks are forms of ordering that are imposed on experience. However, the Republicans benefited from the fact that the two frameworks define and delimit experiences of different logical types. *A New Beginning* occluded the boundaries that demarcated natural and social frames by merging the various televisual genres that conformed to one or the other.

A New Beginning adeptly provided an interpretive frame for its version of social reality. Symbolic signs such as myths, clichés, and formulaic commonplaces were important as suasory devices that repeated, underscored, and dramatized the version of reality proposed by the "natural" signs. Images of the sunrise, the flag being raised, and building construction were provided with a pragmatic context through their juxtaposition with "people on the street" who applauded rising patriotism and declining unemployment. Overall, the film established its credibility with the natural signs, and then worked in social signs that became indistinguishable from the natural.

Although television is obviously a mediation, it is often believed to have the ability to reflect reality. Different television genres are perceived to reflect reality more than others. By mixing genres, *A New Beginning* confused what was typically interpreted as fact or fiction, performance or reality, and even history or legend. Indeed, the confusion was such that there seemed to be no difference. Highly symbolic images, even those that were trite, clichéd, and sentimental, suggested renewal; at the same time, they were anchored in reality because they blended seamlessly with images that would typically be interpreted as unmediated. In *A New Beginning*, the Republicans made a claim that was almost impossible to substantiate: that America was undergoing an economic and spiritual rebirth. They made this claim appear credible through the artful sequencing of scenes and choice of images.

Scenes 10 and 11 aptly demonstrate the confusion of the filmic conventions through which viewers interpret different genres of televisual discourse. In scene 10, elderly Americans voice their support for Ronald Reagan, after which Reagan looks squarely at the camera and states, "There is no threat, from anyone, certainly not from this administration, to Social Security." Social Security was a sensitive issue, as the president's proposals to change the system early in his first term had been greeted with alarm by the elderly. The literal sense of Social Security is quickly undermined, however, by the introduction of another connotation of the term; that is, the safety of society and most specifically, the safety of its president. Reagan's unexpectedly direct policy statement on Social Security is immediately followed by news footage of John Hinckley's 1981 assassination attempt on the president. This brief scene bears all the hallmarks of a "real" news event: the hand-held camera, informal shot composition, poor sound quality, and general confusion. The sequence recycles the popular memory of the assassination attempt, both for those who saw it on television and for those who remember the event but did not "see" it.

The use of techniques and images characteristic of news and documentary help this scene to be perceived as real and plausible. Images appear in an alternating pattern: Reagan is the on-camera narrator who speaks, followed by still photographs that corroborate his words. For example, footage of the assassination attempt dissolves to a close-up of Reagan who speaks to the camera as he recollects the event. His words are supported by a cut to newspaper headlines that report "Reagan Wounded," and then a sequence of photographs that show the president after he was shot. Their use, signaling objectivity and authenticity, strongly reminds the viewer of the "actuality" of the event.[4]

The newspaper photographs of the president dissolve back to the serene, on-camera narrator. Reagan recalls that a doctors' meeting was just concluding as he entered the hospital. Cut to a still photograph of the recuperating Reagan. He stands above an assembly of hospital staff members, their figures dwarfed by an enormous get-well banner on the rear wall. Back to Reagan on-camera, where he repeats the famous joke he purportedly made upon entering the hospital: "Sure, when I saw all those doctors around me too, I said I hoped they were all Republicans." In a rare moment of reflexivity, the film crew's off-camera laughter can be heard. The joke testifies to Reagan's personal strength and makes him seem to be one of the people, just as the film crew's responsive laughter humanizes the narrator and makes him appear to be just another character on film. Reagan is depicted as both larger than life and human, thus setting the stage for his meeting with Cardinal Cooke where he announces his spiritual rebirth.

The camera cuts to a still photograph of Reagan conversing with the late Cardinal Cooke. Reagan then appears on-camera and uses the cardinal's words to imply that he, like America, has been "reborn." He reports, "And we were talking about some of the, call them coincidences that had happened at the time of the shooting and that I had heard after I'd started to recover. And he said that in view of them, God must have been sitting on my shoulder." Reagan concludes by surmising, "Well, must have been. I told him that whatever time I've got left, it now belongs to . . . someone else." His finger points upward. He then pauses reflectively, and significance of his words is underscored by maudlin violin music. The musical accompaniment lends the scene a melodramatic quality characteristic of fiction or a commercial rather than news or documentary.

Throughout this scene, images believed to be representations of actual events merge seamlessly with set-pieces designed solely for a television audience. Though Ronald Reagan was not known as a religious man, he is cast as virtually a Christ-figure: a part-human, part-divine hero who has confronted death, emerged stronger and wiser, and been transformed into America's spiritual leader. Because the boundaries between different representational genres are unclear, this message appears credible, and its fictional qualities may have gone unnoticed.

Occluding Boundaries between Levels

The Republicans conveyed their version of reality by manipulating the television frame as well as by merging the boundaries that differentiated genres of televisual discourse. Television, like Bateson's description of play, is a second-order experience that is abstract and paradoxical. According to Bateson, acts that are framed as play are simulations of first-order "mood" signs, or denotative signs.[5] In play, these are "bracketed" and given an "as-if" status. So, for example, two playing dogs may simulate a fight by using a growl, a denotative sign. The growl is bracketed; it both is and is not what it represents. Television, too, simulates first-order experiences by using denotative signs that both are and are not what they represent. Television re-presents the first-order events it appears to denote. Events portrayed on television are fantasies in that they communicate a reality that does not exist other than through its representation. Moreover, television's representations are mythic in that they transform what may be unfamiliar and threatening into a framework that is coherent and reassuring.[6]

In fact, television's messages are framed as dis-play. Unlike play, where denotative events are assigned an as-if status, television messages are simulations that purport to be presentations. Their as-if status is ignored. Televisual dis-plays become spectacles; they are performances of the real. In consequence, the "real" becomes a simulation, a fantasy, a pseudoevent. The significance of events is influenced, even partially determined, by the televisual frame.

Generic frames provide television events with meaning; these frames, however, are themselves delimited by the television medium, which implicitly works to establish the authenticity of its messages. Paradoxically, words, symbols, and images both are and are not perceived to be what they represent. Framing these messages as fact avoids paradox by equating the representation with what is represented; framing these as fiction also avoids paradox. Fictional, explicitly mediated images can be equated with the ideas or attitudes they connote. The metacommunicative messages that distinguish "live" events, or news, at one extreme, and fictional constructs such as advertisements, at the other, imply different interpretive frames for these genres of televisual discourse.

In *A New Beginning*, however, factual and fictional frames became indistinguishable. By communicating through television, the Republicans pointed to the constructed nature of the discourse. But by merging forms and genres of televisual discourse, messages conventionally interpreted to be real or true (such as news or the Republican National Convention), along with more explicitly symbolic representations, together became framed as "authentic" simulations of reality.

Moreover, because of the similar imagery that pervaded both the videotaped film and the live convention, the film, as a frame for the events it depicted, became virtually indistinguishable from the larger event of which it was a part. Later, these boundaries were further confounded when the Republicans added footage from the convention and rebroadcast the film as a thirty-minute paid commercial. It appeared that the Republicans wanted *A New Beginning* to be perceived as a documentary grounded in reality. Viewers' inability to analyze and decode the complex framing arrangement helped the Republicans attain their goal.

Viewing habits also contributed to the effectiveness of *A New Beginning*. Cinema is the province of the look; but in television, the look is replaced by the glance.[7] People often do not give the medium their full attention. They may watch television while engaged in other activities, or zap and channel-surf at whim. This way of watching increases the possibility that viewers will be taken in by the manipulation of frames.

The three major networks' treatments of the film showed that they too were affected by the manipulation of frames. They did not seem to recognize that the way the film was framed as part of the convention made it difficult to perceive the distinctions between the live versus the filmed events.

Daniel Dayan and Elihu Katz note that networks follow certain implicit rules when they broadcast conventions and other live, though made for television, events.[8] For one, the narrators recede into the background and do not dominate the event. Their commentary is unobtrusive so that the event takes precedence. Ideally, their voices become inseparable from the televised event, so that their presence does not prevent viewers from becoming immersed in the stream of words and images.

However, CBS announcers tried to prevent the film from taking precedence. They showed only its conclusion, thus keeping the viewers from full involvement. As outside narrators, they were far from unobtrusive. Newscasters Dan Rather and Bill Plante made explicit editorial comments, reminding viewers that the film was part of the Republican campaign strategy. But rather than demystifying the Republicans' ideology, CBS only reinforced perceptions of the film's power.

When CBS showed the film, their shots of the massive video-screen at the Dallas convention hall was literally framed by the live convention in the foreground, filled with cheering conventioneers waving flags and red, white, and blue balloons. Similarly, NBC announcers Tom Brokaw and Roger Mudd discussed the film against the background of the convention floor, hoping to divert attention from the film to the commentary. Instead of downplaying the significance of the film, their remarks, overlaid upon the live event and interspersed between the live event and the film (itself intercut with images of the live convention), prevented the viewers from establishing a clear sense of framing. Consequently, their talk only produced a desire for contact with the pseudodiscourse and images. Their words were quickly overpowered by the immediacy and presence of the words, sounds, and images that constituted the film and the live celebration that was the convention.

NBC was the only network to show the film in its entirety, although they periodically reminded viewers that they were watching a Republican production. Their editorial criticisms were the most scathing. Correspondent Roger Mudd called attention to what was excluded and what was included in the film, presumably to highlight its bias. However, Mudd's attack merely served to define a negative background against which *A New Beginning* could be more clearly perceived.

NBC's broadcast of the film was intercut with several reaction shots of the viewing crowd projected on the huge screen at the convention arena. This device was presumably meant to prevent the home viewer from becoming immersed in the film and to call attention to it as an orchestrated televisual event. In fact, the crowd shots may have had the opposite effect, making the live convention virtually indistinguishable from the film itself, and further merging and confusing different levels of mediation. Confusion only increased when NBC's cameras showed Ronald Reagan arriving at the convention hall in time to watch himself on television.

The NBC cameras even contributed, albeit inadvertently, to the effective transition from the penultimate to the concluding scene of the film. They cut away from the film, where American service flags and banners were onscreen, to the convention floor. There, conventioneers were watching the videoscreen in the background; in the foreground, a large American flag was waved in response to the film. The cameras returned to their coverage just in time to capture a shot of a policeman hoisting a flag, the repetition stressing the continuity between the film and the convention. The convention became part of the film that was part of the convention, and the convention's perceived qualities of liveness, immediacy, and authenticity became associated with the perceived authority of the film.

ABC took yet another approach to the Reagan film. Announcer Jeff Greenfield contrasted the Reagan and Mondale films, analyzing excerpts from each. Freeze-frames from both films were compared on a split videoscreen. The Statue of Liberty, for instance, appeared in both films; yet in the Reagan film the statue's reconstruction symbolized a broader rebuilding of America and American spirit. The White House appeared in both films, although in *A New Beginning*, shots of the building dissolved into images of Ronald Reagan at home in the Oval Office. This attempt to disempower the event, like that of CBS and NBC, only emphasized the Republicans' more sophisticated use of imagery and symbolism.

Unifying Frames

Besides occluding genres and levels of discourse, framing also suc-
ceeded in diminishing the distance between the televised image and
the viewer. The voice and figure of Ronald Reagan created a sense of
presence and intimacy with the viewer, and provided the unifying
point of reference for all of the different levels of representation.
Reagan was the subject of both the film and the convention; he was
also narrator and a character within the film. As such, he was an
image, or simulation, who resolved contradictions between intimacy
and authority, identification and distance.

The narrator in both film and television is perceived to be the
voice of truth who organizes all of the discourses that make up the
visual text.[9] By directly or indirectly addressing an audience, both the
narrator and characters in a film convey the impression of discourse,
although it is the narrator who is guarantor of its truth. Ronald
Reagan as narrator appeared to be the voice of truth; he unified different levels of representation characterized according to their modes
of address.

Television's modes of address are conceptualized in terms of lin-
guist Emile Benveniste' distinctions of "histoire" and "discourse."[10]
Histoire, or story, is most simply the content or chain of events that
compose a narrative. Discourse, on the other hand, refers to the
means by which the story is communicated, its metalinguistic message. Discourse always implies an "I" and a "you"; it involves a
source who shapes a message for a receiver. Though histoire and discourse are inseparable aspects of film and television, narrative cinema is typically believed to be histoire without discourse, a story
unfolding without an enunciative source. Like film, television as histoire appears to be impersonal speech without a speaker, which
reflects reality. Yet as discourse, which involves a speaker taking
responsibility for her utterances, it creates the impression of dialogue,
of a conversation between a speaker and listener.

A New Beginning merged the boundaries that differentiate story
and discourse. In regard to television, histoire and discourse may be
conceived as spaces that set up a particular relationship between
images and audience.[11] The story-space of television gives the
impression of unmediated events appearing before an audience,
while discourse-space mimics face-to-face conversation, where a
speaker dialogues with an audience. With television, discourse and

story-space overlap, so that television gives an impression, or "fiction of discourse." Television's admixture of story and discourse, and the consequent role of the narrator as enunciative source of authority, is apparent throughout *A New Beginning*. The televisual narrator creates the impression of discourse, of an enunciation that defines an "I" and implies a "you." That this "I" is a simulation is of little consequence; as in the case of Ronald Reagan, the image is the reality. Most important, this is possible because the frame that separates televisual reality from the viewer is dissolved.

The voice and figure of Ronald Reagan unified the spaces of discourse and histoire in *A New Beginning* in order to create a fiction of discourse that was familiar and reassuring to the viewer. As both narrator and character in the film, the image of Ronald Reagan both defined and was defined by the various scenes throughout the film. Similarly, the resultant fiction of discourse both constituted and was constituted by the viewing audience outside of the film.

The film begins in story-space that is framed in the past. Reagan's 1980 Inaugural Address and images of America and its citizens are intercut with one another, linked by a common musical theme. However, the priority of the inauguration is asserted; the voices of Ronald Reagan and the Chief Justice reiterating the oath of office provide the voice-over narration for the otherwise unrelated images that compose the scene. The inauguration, which occupies the discursive-space of the entire scene, has authority because it is associated with a prior reality, the past where the event "really" happened.

In scene 2, Reagan moves from character to narrator, from indirect story-space to the direct address that constitutes discursive-space. The images of both the inauguration and America dissolve into the White House, marking the end of the first scene. Reagan's "live" off-camera voice retrospectively frames the opening, as he directly addresses the audience and explains its significance: "Yes, it was quite a day . . . a new beginning."

Throughout scene 2, Reagan's voice remains off-camera. Discursive- and story-space overlap, as the visual images constitute histoire and the voice-over functions as discourse. Reagan is a narrator who describes his presidential duties; at the same time, he is a character who acts on screen. As narrator, he establishes a discursive relation with his audience, although as character he is not aware of its existence. He takes on dual roles here, although his role as narrator is perceived to be more authoritative. For instance, when Reagan the narrator asserts that his job is not lonely, Reagan the character works alone at his desk. The picture belies the words, which supports the image of Ronald Reagan to reinforce his modest stoicism. His role as narrator authenticates and renders coherent the fictional story-space, but the story-space, too, supports his position as narrator. The inter-relation of character and narrator constitutes the resultant image of Ronald Reagan.

In scene 2, also, Reagan's voice is established as the institutional voice of *A New Beginning*, the voice of authority, distinguished from other, subordinate voices throughout the film.[12] In fact, Nancy Reagan's position is so subordinate in the film that although she appears in many scenes throughout the film, she does not speak. She has no voice.

Institutionalized narrators directly address the camera; they carry the most authority when they are perceived to be in live, studio situations. Bush is located in the White House, which serves as the studio-space throughout the film. Yet, if this space is authoritative, it is not the province of George Bush. When he appears in scene 3, he does not directly address the camera. Bush indirectly addresses the viewing audience, glancing off to the side as he speaks to an invisible interviewer. His authority is also subverted by visual means: as he speaks, the background of the shot depicts the backside of a horse pointed in his face. Such a visual gaffe may not have been intentional, but it is an example of the excess meaning that images and texts contain.

Bush is followed by a series of interviews with "ordinary Americans" who attest to spiritual and economic renewal. None of these people directly face the camera. They provide support for Ronald Reagan by testifying to the veracity of the themes already introduced. Their positions are coded as less authoritative than that of George Bush. They are interviewed "on the street," in actuality rather than in the White House. They are easily identified types interviewed against backgrounds that help to locate them socially. These interviewees are placed in actuality, and their mode of address is indirect. They are securely within the realm of story-space that is framed and rendered coherent by the film's narrator, Ronald Reagan. In fact, they were not "ordinary Americans," with all that this term implies. Reagan's campaign managers reported in a *Life* magazine interview that they were friends of Republican campaign workers—not exactly a random sample.[13]

The last person interviewed serves as a transition to scene 5; his voice is entirely functional. Scene 5 is the most clearly articulated story-space of the entire film. It is pure spectacle: a song where country singer Lee Greenwood croons, "I'm proud to be an American." This song was later nominated for a Grammy Award and became a music video whose images mimicked this scene of the film, an example of how the genres within the film echoed, recalled, and collapsed into other cultural forms. In the context of *A New Beginning*, however, the song constructs the fantasy of the film. All of its themes and images appear in this sequence: rebirth, renewal, pride, patriotism, optimism, work, faith, family, and peace. Throughout the film, images recall and repeat these themes; they are reiterated by both characters and the narrator, Ronald Reagan. They become integrated into the discursive space of the film, as the fantasy becomes framed by "reality."

Ronald Reagan's voice, predictably, bridges this sequence to scene 6, where he relates America's reawakening of pride and patriotism to the military. Here again, he is both narrator and character as his offscreen voice describes the images within the frame. This double figure serves as illustrative proof of the humanity tempered by authority of "Ronald Reagan"; that is, Ronald Reagan as both character and narrator, as one of the people and a leader who is above them, as he appears inside and outside of the film. His character even breaks into the discourse of the narrator here, as character Reagan remarks that the food on his cafeteria tray "looks good." He does not directly address the audience, but the combination of both voices indicates the unity of character and narrator, and the fiction of discourse that is *A New Beginning*.

Not until scene 8 does Reagan directly address his audience on-camera with a report on economic improvements since he has been in office. His function as organizer of story-space is apparent here; as he speaks, corroborative images flash onscreen. Newspaper headlines that say "A Break in Interest Rates" move laterally across the frame, followed by a family moving into a home with a "Sold" sign in front of it. Reagan orders and organizes all of the images that surround him; he conjures them and makes them "exist." His voice and figure authenticate them; at the same time, these images support his discourse.

As the film progresses, Ronald Reagan takes on a more prominent role as narrator, firmly establishing his position of authority. He directly addresses his audience from the White House, and "the people" who spoke for themselves earlier in the film during interviews appear less and less frequently. Ronald Reagan, both character and narrator, speaks for himself. Throughout the film, Reagan takes on a variety of roles, as he shifts in and out of direct address, and in and out of discourse- and story-space. In this way Ronald Reagan as character and narrator frame each other and unify the space of story and discourse.

In the replay of the assassination attempt in scene 11, for instance, Reagan is first presented as a character, located in actuality, who is not aware of the viewing audience outside of the film. His voice-over narration accompanies news footage and still photographs. Then he appears as a live character/narrator who directly addresses his audience. The scene begins in story-space but ends in discursive-space. But there is also a more powerful effect. In this scene, the character transforms into the narrator in the same way, and at the same time, that the "human" Ronald Reagan is transformed to the "divine." "Ronald Reagan," after this, represents the unified realms of story and discourse. During the following scenes, covering his diplomatic missions to Japan and China, he is man of peace, empowered to unify opposites such as East and West.

Later, as he presides over the D-Day commemoration ceremony in Normandy, character and narrator became merged, as Reagan shifts back and forth, almost imperceptibly, from the character of president to the omniscient narrator outside the event who is able to comment on it. The scene begins with a high-angle shot of cliffs overlooking the ocean. Reagan's offscreen voice locates the viewer: "We stand on a lonely windswept point on the northern shore of France." The camera cuts and then pans left across a group of sixty-two elderly men seated outdoors near the edge of the water. It stops at the figure of Ronald Reagan, who stands before them. The words, it turns out, have a double function. They address the home viewing audience, and they are part of his speech to the D-Day veterans. The offscreen narrator effortlessly becomes the onscreen character.

In the next shot, Reagan reasserts his narrative authority. As recalls D-Day in the speech, his words are accompanied by archival footage of American troops landing in Normandy. When he recalls the sound of gunfire, the viewer hears the "actual" sounds of the battle. The camera cuts and once again pans the faces of the men at the commemoration ceremony. Reagan's narratorial voice breaks in, accompanied by instrumental music, which cues the viewer that he is now commenting upon the event from a position outside. At this point, Reagan the narrator recalls the speech at Normandy rather than D-Day itself. "It was a very moving experience," he emphasizes. He then commends the veterans, although the images show not the onscreen veterans, but the cemetery at Normandy. Solemn music plays as close-, medium-, and long-shots of crosses marked by American flags fill the screen. The outside narrator's voice remarks, "these are the products of the freest society the world has ever known."

The camera cuts to Reagan at a podium, again a character/narrator, as he gives a second speech at Normandy. Here he narrates a letter sent to him by a young woman, Lisa Zanatta Henn, who mourns her father, a recently deceased D-Day veteran. The evocative power of his narratorial voice is supported by a strong visual image as well as music that underscores the emotional pull of the scene. As a high-angle shot captures the woman's sobs, thus emphasizing her vulnerability, Reagan once again becomes narrator outside of the event. Then the camera cuts back to him reading at the podium. He slips back into character as his voice chokes with emotion. It is this power of the narrator to recall, reorder, and reorganize actual events that conveys the "truth" of the fiction of discourse, while the character provides a point of identification for the viewing audience. This scene, more than any other in the film, demonstrates Reagan's ability to unify character and narrator, story and discourse, in the service of ideology. It ends with Reagan the character/narrator making a plea for stronger defense: "We may always be prepared so that we may always be free."

Following the remarkable D-Day scene, the voice of the narrator, having already established its authenticity and authority, provides Ronald Reagan's own biography; that is, establishes the "character" of the character. This scene highlights Reagan's mode of presentation, which is expertly "discursive." He was not only an actor, but a professional narrator who knew how to address television audiences. Reagan's voice was warm, conversational, and apparently sincere; he came across as "just a regular guy." This was the character he cultivated in his film roles, and which he continued to cultivate as president of the United States.

The film concludes with a reiteration of the fantasy of *A New Beginning*. Lee Greenwood sings the refrain of "God Bless the USA," accompanied by a repetition of images of American resurgence and a final still photograph of Ronald Reagan with his hands clasped over his head in a victory sign.

As Greenwood's song ended, the story-space of the film

merged into the "real" world of the Republican National Convention. Applause for the film became chants for Ronald Reagan, and viewers were greeted by yet another image of the president. This time, the "live" Ronald Reagan gave his acceptance address for the Republican Party's nomination, culminating both the film and the convention. Ronald Reagan, the speaker, became framed by the convention, which he simultaneously framed. The new fiction of discourse created by the event secured the image of Ronald Reagan in the present, a figure that unified genres, levels, and spaces of televisual discourse.

The image of Ronald Reagan also defined the viewer whom it addressed. Reagan's position was that of authority, of knowledge. In creating a fiction of discourse, he also created the fiction of participation. The viewer he addressed was a consumer, a receiver of preconstructed meanings. Television presented a myth, a story, a spectacle of discourse that claimed to represent a real world outside of its frame. The viewer became subjected to an imaginary relationship, a fiction of discourse. But Ronald Reagan's fiction comforted and cajoled; he gave the American people the image they wanted to see.

3 Ronald Reagan and the Conservative Movement

Still, the overriding issues of this election were almost certainly economic and imperial-maintenance issues, with the former the more important. Perhaps the most durable interest most voters have is the maintenance of the "American Dream" itself: the promise of a better life, and particularly the promise of a better life for one's children. . . . Ronald Reagan promised above all that the American Dream could be revitalized. Perhaps even more important, he projected a boundless faith and optimism that the traditional ways could work; and in this, stood in sharp contrast to a Carter whose message appeared to be gloomy, pessimistic, and confused.
—Walter Dean Burnham, "The 1980 Earthquake"

A New Beginning was the Republicans' most comprehensive presentation of Ronald Reagan and his political message during the 1984 presidential campaign. Whether considered to be news, a documentary, an advertisement, or propaganda, the mediated record of the aims and accomplishments of the Reagan Administration offered Ronald Reagan and his rhetorical vision to the American public. The juxtaposition of words, sounds, and images—some news, some staged for the film, some both—reinforced the message of rebirth initiated during the 1980 campaign.

The film's form, content, and framing were highly selective. The result emphasized aspects of the world according to Reagan's ideology, and ignored those that did not indicate a renewed and revitalized American self-image. Reagan's vision appeared tenable to the viewers addressed by the film. The majority of voting Americans, in 1980 and again in 1984, voiced their support by providing him with consecutive landslide victories. These landslides were particularly significant because prior to 1980 the Democrats had been the party of the middle and working classes who made up the political majority in the United States. Ronald Reagan came to power by representing the Republicans as the party of the majority and the party of change. This enabled him to secure many traditionally Democratic votes, and led to a new conservative political era.

A New Beginning articulated Reagan's political ideology, framed it as reality, and promulgated it largely through symbolic appeals to pride, patriotism, and prosperity. The film, like the entire 1984 campaign, lacked substantive argument and specific policy rationales, even though the Reagan administration's policies implemented some of the most radical changes in government since Roosevelt's New Deal programs. By couching his political objectives in themes and images that spoke to the political majority, Reagan shifted party alliances to the right and redefined the political agenda of the United States.

Ronald Reagan led the movement against the social philosophy, economic theory, and political ideology of the liberal democratic "welfare state." Liberalism, as represented by Carter and Mondale, had dominated American politics since Roosevelt's 1933 New Deal, even when Republican presidents were in office. One technique Reagan used to shift the majority of Americans from a liberal to a conservative frame was the use of rebirth rhetoric, which symbolically addressed social, political, and personal concerns of the times, rather than by specifically outlining political aims and objectives.

Liberal Theory and Practice Prior to Reagan's Presidency

Carter and Mondale's liberal social philosophy, economic theory, and political ideology were grounded in the social changes wrought by industrialization and the emergence of the market economy. With industrialization, which began roughly in the post-Civil War period, the United States gradually was transformed from an agrarian economy to one dominated by self-regulating market forces. Ideally, the self-regulating market, based upon the values of freedom, equality, and just exchange, would produce the "good society."[1]

However, the self-regulating market produced a consumer society as a consequence of industrialization and mass production of goods and services. Emphasis shifted from production to consumption as a greater quantity and diversity of products became available. Economic relations were no longer predicated on the belief that work was rewarded with self-fulfillment; instead, fulfillment was relegated to the sphere of consumption. In effect, capitalism became dissociated from the Protestant ethic, which equated work with virtue. Traditional values no longer applied to the modern world.

Not only did the self-regulating market fail to produce the good society with liberty and affluence for all, but the subsequent periods of boom or bust produced greater social inequality and instability. Eventually, America faced the Great Depression of 1929. Franklin Delano Roosevelt's liberal New Deal attempted to restore social order by making major structural changes in government and the economy. Roosevelt also recognized the need to affect basic values in order to achieve change (as did Reagan, years later). The policies instituted during Roosevelt's presidency not only restructured the market economy, but established the modern democratic liberal welfare state and the values that sustained it.

Initially, the intervention of government as manager of industry, agriculture, and the economy was intended to produce economic growth and prosperity in response to the Depression. During World War II, the centralized role of government became intertwined with Keynesian economic theory and the "planned" economy. This theory, which became increasingly accepted by both Democratic and Republican presidents after Roosevelt, assumed that supply creates demand: briefly stated, technological innovations and the continuing availability of new goods and services satisfy demand, provide employment, and lead to economic growth.

During the period of increased industrialization and technological progress that followed the war, government regulations ensured that, with the proliferation of technological developments, supply did not exceed demand and demands could be satisfied. Government's role in maintaining economic and technological growth increased, as did its role as provider of social, economic, and personal well-being. The self-regulating market could not fulfill the promises of capitalism, so the government took over this task. Liberals saw consumerism as the engine of capitalism, and therefore aimed to establish a generalized middle class, with increased personal freedom, equality, and material prosperity. Such an aim was accompanied by an emphasis upon the democratic and egalitarian aspects of capitalism. Liberal policies were responsible for entitlement programs, such as Social Security and unemployment insurance, as well as Medicare, Medicaid, and welfare. Through the years, government grants and student loans made it possible for the economically deprived to attend college. After mass movements in the 1960s, legislation was passed to assure civil rights and equality of opportunity for minority groups.

Crisis of Liberalism

The two decades prior to 1980 were periods of great social turbulence and political unrest. With the market economy, legitimacy was based on the belief that the market itself was the means to the good society; with liberalism, legitimacy was based on belief in government's authority to make decisions. This belief would be questioned in the sixties and on into the next decade. In the public realm, the liberal welfare state, with its Keynesian economic theory, centralized government, and bureaucracy, was increasingly perceived to be in a state of crisis. Ronald Reagan attacked the core of liberalism when he said, in his now-famous words, "Government is not the solution to the problem, government is the problem."[2]

Reagan blamed economic problems upon the highly centralized government bureaucracy, with its increased responsibilities for individual welfare and for regulation of business and industry to assure economic growth. A worldwide price revolution during the 1970s, coupled with the inflationary effects of excessive government defense and domestic spending during the Johnson years, resulted in an economic recession. Increased unemployment and high interest rates prevented middle-income people from purchasing homes or cars, and there was little speculation or investment as people tried to save rather than spend. The economy, dependent on investment, expansion, and consumption, was stagnating. While liberalism may have worked during the period when America was becoming industrialized, the new postindustrial era of inflation, limited resources, and unemployment suggested to many that the welfare state did not work. Americans paid increasingly high taxes for government programs, such as welfare, which essentially aimed to create equality for all through more equitable distribution and use of wealth and resources. The middle classes, in particular, became increasingly resentful at seeing their tax dollars funding government programs from which they seemed to gain little or nothing.

Not only were the middle classes ready to rail against the liberal welfare state, but the American presidency as an institution was in a state of disarray when Ronald Reagan came on the scene. The

Watergate affair, and the perceived lack of leadership skills displayed by Presidents Ford and Carter, led to a growing crisis of authority and lack of faith in the institution itself. Political theorist James Barber has noted that Ford's pollsters advised him in 1976 that Americans wanted a president to demonstrate "moral leadership, strength of character, religious conviction, love of family, and personal integrity above all else."[3] However, Ford's inability to project leadership, and Carter's subsequent disappointments led to an estimated 80 percent of Americans who, in 1979, believed that the country was on the wrong track.[4] By 1980, people were looking for a leader with confidence and charisma. Enter Ronald Reagan.

Patriotic sentiments were also on the wane prior to the Reagan presidency. The crisis of confidence in government was induced partly by the Vietnam War and partly from the knowledge that America no longer dominated the world economically or militarily as it had in the 1950s. Defeat in Vietnam, the increasing economic power of the OPEC nations, the overthrow of the American-backed Shah of Iran followed by American impotence during the hostage crisis in Teheran, Carter's surrender of rights to the Panama Canal, Central American turmoil, and the continuing cold war with the Soviet Union: all perpetuated American fears of Communism and the loss of individual freedom which it implied. American loss of prestige abroad was reflected in the public attitude at home.

A changing social and moral climate also set the stage for political events in the 1980s.[5] The tumultuous sixties were marked by civil rights, gay, and feminist movements for equality. Students organized on the left to protest the Vietnam War; many rejected the materialistic ethic that had motivated their parents and opted for alternative values and life-styles. The liberal emphasis upon secular and humanistic values placed the individual, rather than any absolute authority, at the center of the moral universe. This "crisis" in traditional values provoked a conservative reaction in the seventies and on into the eighties; it was largely responsible for the emergence of the New Right, a group of religious leaders who mobilized politically to combat the perceived immorality of liberal policies.

Reagan capitalized on a conservative backlash to what was perceived to be an overly permissive society. The cornerstones of capitalism—the traditional American values of patriotism, the nuclear family, religious faith and the work ethic—were felt to be threatened, and the new conservatism centered around the restoration of these values. The time was right for Reagan's affirmative rhetoric of renewal to reclaim traditional American values and frame them as the province of conservative Republicans. By 1984, he had become inextricably linked to the restoration of American values, along with social, economic, patriotic, and military resurgence. "There's a whole new attitude in America today. And I think that needs to be continued," says one representative black man in the campaign film. Not surprisingly, patriotism, religion, work, a strong defense, and the nuclear family are recurrent themes and images in *A New Beginning*.

Most likely the interaction of personal, social, political, and economic factors, rather than the dominance of one or the other, set the stage for Ronald Reagan and the conservative movement to shift the United States to the conservative right in the 1980s. Many people were disenchanted with liberalism, and the country was experiencing stresses and strains in many areas. Just as for most people these "crises" were experienced but not articulated, Reagan addressed many of them implicitly. While the content of his rhetoric focused upon new economic prosperity, his themes, imagery, and nonverbal communication spoke to patriotism and traditional values. Reagan's rebirth rhetoric offered secular salvation, a symbolic resolution of personal and public crises.

However, Reagan's rhetoric only created the appearance of renewal and revitalization. He merged the personal and political, ethics and economics, myth and theory, in order to achieve change. By doing so, the Republicans, through Ronald Reagan, were able to frame a cohesive and positive reality for the American voters, an illusory reality far more palatable than the darker vision depicted by liberal Democrats Jimmy Carter and Walter Mondale.

Rebirth of Populism

Ronald Reagan's rhetorical appeals attempted to renew popular faith in the ideals of capitalism by affirming traditional American values and their manifestation in myths such as those of the individual, the community, and the American Dream. If successful, this merger of myth and theory would allow him to instate his version of the market economy and effectively redirect the course of American government and society. Reagan realized his aims through use of rebirth rhetoric that resonated with American populism and religious fundamentalism.

Reagan's economic reforms were linked to populist themes. He urged a return to the free-enterprise, self-regulating market economy, which was based upon the populist assumptions that individualism, private incentives, and traditional values (such as equality of opportunity, self-help tempered by good-neighborliness, and even patriarchal sex roles) were necessary to create the good society.

Populist movements, rooted in the Declaration of Independence, have historically been concerned with asserting individual rights, free from any outside (especially governmental) interference. Populism is often related to Jacksonian democracy, which emphasized the common person. Jacksonian democracy and the populist movement that grew out of it were committed to the ideals of liberty, equality, and pursuit of happiness as the fundamental rights of all Americans. The populist vision was of a struggle between the common man and powerful interests (either corporate, or in Reagan's case, bureaucratic) that threaten to encroach upon the individual.[6]

Most important, Reagan's use of populist rhetoric corresponded with the values required in a free-market economy. The central populist doctrine of self-help emphasized individualism and equality of opportunity as the necessary conditions for the pursuit of happiness. It was the individual's responsibility, not society's, to improve his or her own condition. Needless to say, this directly contradicted the liberal assumption that it was society's responsibility to improve the individual's condition, and that inequalities were the result of the system rather than due to individual defects. Reagan promoted the populist idea that individuals who were willing and determined to succeed economically could do so if they were unimpeded by the government.

Not only did Ronald Reagan espouse populist principles, but in so doing he reaffirmed the myths of small-town America and the moral concerns associated with the New Right. Populism and evangelical and fundamentalist religious movements have typically been based in rural regions in America, and these movements have been related to major social and political changes. Reagan, seeking to mobilize popular support in order to make major changes, sought to create a consensus of "the people," the generalized middle. By pointing to (and in a sense, constituting) the failure of liberalism and its values, Reagan was able to establish a new majority consisting of those traditional, small-town (in spirit, if not in reality), "ordinary" Americans.[7]

Reagan's populism enabled him to gather the traditionally Democratic majority of middle and working classes under the

Republican banner. Reagan needed to secure their support, particularly those located in the southern and midwestern Sunbelt states whose Electoral College votes would secure him a landslide victory. In 1980 and again in 1984, Reagan supporters formed a coalition of those otherwise disparate Americans who had been disillusioned with the course and direction that America was taking, and who wanted to believe that Ronald Reagan, the new captain of their ship, was able to steer them to the promised land.

The Reagan Resolution

Ronald Reagan's assault against the liberal welfare state took place in the context of severe American disaffection, if not actual crisis. His conservatism was based upon the premise that liberal solutions do not work; in his view, attempts to provide equality and privilege regardless of individual productivity led to lethargy and dependency on government. Reagan's political ideology offered an alternative that ostensibly resolved the "crisis." His positions were not new in 1980. Since the 1960s he had been lashing out against centralized government and liberal policies and programs, which he held responsible for personal and public malaise.

One of Reagan's most basic beliefs was that to solve current problems, the size and power of the federal government must be reduced. His position corresponded to what has been termed "Jeffersonian Republicanism": it involved decentralization in the form of deregulation of industry and debureaucratization of society (like Jefferson), a return to the free-market economy (a Republican position), and a maximization of individual responsibility, making "enlightened self-interest" the prime mover in relations of exchange.[8] Thus, in 1980 Reagan advocated less government control of states and industries; cutting inflation by decreasing government spending; balancing the federal budget (a goal he would later abandon); reducing income taxes to stimulate the economy; rebuilding a strong America by increasing defense spending; and maintaining American interests abroad by intervening in Third World countries.

In addition, Reagan offered a specific plan for economic change in 1980 that became known as Reaganomics. This plan further assisted his cause with the voting public who was looking for answers Democrat Jimmy Carter did not seem able to provide. Prior to Reagan's 1980 election campaign, he had become an adherent of "supply-side economics," a theory which became the thrust of his election bid. Reagan's plan was a radical departure from both Republican and Democratic policies since the New Deal, which incurred the wrath of more moderate Republicans, like George Bush, who referred to it as "voodoo economics." Reagan's plan was a synthesis of supply-side economics, or the theory of deep tax cuts, along with minimal government regulation of private enterprise and monetarism (limiting the money supply in order to decrease inflation and budget deficits). Despite the fact that supply-side economics and monetarism were not necessarily compatible, this program was intended to provide the conditions for optimal economic growth and prosperity.

Simply stated, the theory of deep tax cuts was based upon the assumption that demand created supply. To increase productivity and assure economic growth, policies had to increase both the demand for productive material, such as people, land, or machines, and also increase people's incentive to work. The idea was that removing government barriers to productivity, most notably high taxes, accomplished this. Supply-siders also blamed welfare programs for reducing incentive to work, especially since with high taxes people could earn almost as much on welfare as they would earn in after-tax income. Thus, the across-the-board tax cuts that Reagan advocated were supposed to increase productivity because workers would be able to keep more of the money they earned. In turn, workers having more money would instigate more investments and business enterprises, which would then create more jobs, which would result in economic growth. Few people claimed to understand the as-yet-untested plan, and many saw its potential for aiding the rich more than the poor. However, in the context of the eighties' postindustrial capitalism, Reagan was able to provide Americans with an alternative to the Democrats' prospectus of austerity and sacrifice. He offered hope and promised economic abundance.

While Reaganomics was an attempt to return to the self-regulating market that characterized the pre-welfare state American economy, there was a pragmatic aspect that suggested it did not solely aim to recover the past. For instance, Reagan retained the liberal notion of economic growth as a social and political goal. This distinguished him from other Republican candidates in 1980. He stressed the need for an economic change that offered prosperity, and prosperity for all. He promised that there would be economic growth for all strata of society. This, too, was an appeal to the majority.

Reagan's political ideology was consistent with the social aims of the New Right, and he did, to some extent, try to reverse liberal policies with legislation that would make abortion illegal and return prayer to the schools. His administration dropped affirmative-action programs and refused to support the Equal Rights Amendment (ERA), and it reduced Medicare and Medicaid, thus forcing the return of the care of the elderly to the family. While he did advocate reductions or eliminations of many social programs (based upon the rationale that they were wasteful or that, as the economy got better, there would be less need for them), he also retained a safety net of established social programs such as welfare (albeit on a reduced scale), unemployment insurance, and Social Security (although the latter became a somewhat controversial issue). This, no doubt, made the proposed changes less threatening to the middle classes who occasionally had to rely upon such programs, especially as the economy worsened.

Reaganomics was an economic attempt to return America to the pre-liberal market economy, and to return America to the position of military supremacy the country had occupied in the 1950s. Ethically, it claimed to restore the independence and self-reliance of the individual who reaped the material and moral rewards for her labor and initiative. Reagan's evocation of values that were consistent with a market economy enabled him to address, and appear to resolve, social and moral as well as economic issues. By reinstilling faith in the American Dream, and conveying an image of a strong America with a sure leader, he appeared to offer hope that many of the conflicts and contradictions that perplexed the majority of Americans could be resolved.

4   Mythic Rhetoric in *A New Beginning*

*For the most part, the mythmaker does not invent his facts; he
interprets facts which are already given in a culture to which he
belongs. What marks his account as a myth is not its content,
but its dramatic form and the fact that it serves as a practical
argument. Its success as a practical argument depends upon its
being accepted as true, if it explains the experience of those to
whom it is addressed, and justifies the practical purposes they
have in mind.*

—Henry Tudor, Political Myth

Mythic Rhetoric

Ronald Reagan's conservative ideology offered Americans a coherent, unproblematic, self-affirming view of themselves and their country. Moreover, the Republicans' manipulation of interpretive frames
appeared to ground Reagan's vision of strength, hope, and prosperity in reality. In both word and deed, news and advertisements,
Reagan provided reassurance that America, under his leadership,
was spiritually and economically well again, that America was not a
house divided, that there was unity and consensus in support of
Ronald Reagan.

However, Reagan's ideology provides only a partial explanation of his political success. It does not fully account for his over-
whelming appeal to the voting majority of the American people.
Reagan's success may be more fully understood by examining *A New
Beginning* from a mythic frame. The Republicans' use of mythic
rhetoric enabled them to achieve their political aims by appealing to
deep-seated needs and desires of the American people. In particular,
the myth of rebirth expressed their ideology and provided a link
between the personal and the political. Before proceeding, the problematic notion of myth must be clarified; this term is subject to

diverse interpretations that are not always consonant with each other.

Myth is a socially constructed representation of reality that articulates the central beliefs, values, and preoccupations of a culture. Unlike approaches that regard myths as false or illusory beliefs, or even those that propose that myths express universal truths, this analysis is not concerned with explaining whether they are true or false. Since meaning is itself a social construction, so is the reality a myth may express. As social constructions that articulate an interpretive stance, mythic symbolizations can be true, illusory, or both. Depending upon whether one is "inside" or "outside" the myth, it can be viewed as true or illusory, logical or illogical, a synthesis of contradictions or itself contradictory. From the perspective of the reader on the inside, myths are true because they are credible representations of reality. At the same time, from an outside stance, myths are illusory in that they mask their own nature as constructions that may be crafted to serve instrumental purposes.[1]

Myths are constitutive because they create the understanding that they simultaneously impose. They are selective and arbitrary; they offer an interpretation of reality to which there is always an alternative. Further, a society may tolerate contradictory myths. American society is marked by the presence of equally powerful, yet opposing myths. Their coexistence provides a means of dealing with the contradictions that prevail within the society; individuals can adopt whichever opposing version of a myth is necessary to justify themselves or adapt to changing circumstances.[2] What remains, however, is that the work of myth is to deny its own arbitrary stature; thus, the reality that myth articulates appears to be self-evident, a priori, prereflectively true.

Roland Barthes, in *Mythologies*, suggests that myths are metacommunicative forms of discourse; they are the interpretive frames through which the discursive, rhetorical modes of symbolization can be comprehended. Most importantly, myths do not render interpretations of reality meaningful. They naturalize already meaningful interpretations of reality so that these interpretations appear to be absolute, beyond arbitration or negotiation. For example, the television screen depicts an image of Ronald Reagan dressed in army uniform as he sings hymns with soldiers on the front line of the Korean demilitarized zone. When viewers interpret this image, they naturally associate Ronald Reagan with freedom, patriotism, religiosity, military strength, and camaraderie. Viewers have already learned these associations prior to seeing the image; as myths, they appear to be total, irrefutable, unquestioned. Myths then appear to represent reality; they are ideological. For this reason, even when intention is discerned behind the presence of a myth, it is not necessarily rejected as false or illusory.

Myths then are frames that simultaneously form and represent social reality. Further, myths can be put forth to serve the interests of a society or a group within it while appearing not to do so. The myth of rebirth that Ronald Reagan invoked in *A New Beginning*, for example, served to justify the American creed, to forge a common identity, and to define a sense of national purpose. Its motive was reaffirmation: to revitalize and redefine American self-images in accordance with the interests of his conservative ideology.[3] The campaign film was a vehicle through which the myth of rebirth, linked to the accomplishments of the Reagan administration, was presented to the viewing audience in the dramatic form of televised history. The film both constructed and reinforced the central Republican myth, or interpretive frame, of a new beginning, in which America's problems, struggles, and strife would be overcome with Ronald Reagan as president.

The myth of rebirth has its roots in Western religion. Rebirth is based upon the Edenic idea of an idyllic past that has been lost but can be regained. In American history, it provided the form for the Puritan jeremiad sermons, which assumed that the Puritans were the Chosen People and America was the Promised Land. The people were admonished by a minister-prophet that although they had erred, if they repented the Promised Land would be restored.[4]

Its secular version became prevalent as social and political concerns replaced religious ones. The myth then posited that America was the Promised Land of liberty and freedom for all; though people may have fallen away from its fundamental principles, right actions would help the country to fulfill its destiny. Politicians have invoked this myth throughout American history, either to explain that current suffering and strife will be alleviated, or if things are going well, to suggest that the ideal world is at hand. The Reagan film's nostalgic evocation of a simple, harmonious past and its emphasis upon unity, consensus, and reconciliation in the present both recalled and replayed the American myth of rebirth. Though its vision of rebirth was secular, the film was sprinkled with religious references: as noted above, Reagan attends an outdoor church service and prays with American servicemen in Korea. In other scenes, he claims that

God was sitting on his shoulder during the assassination attempt, walks with Nancy among the crosses that mark the graves of those who died in Normandy, and closely paraphrases the first verse of Psalm 121 towards the end of the film.[5]

A New Beginning can usefully be considered a rhetorical ritual that both evoked and itself enacted the myth of rebirth in order to orient the political majority to Republican frames of mind. According to James Hoban, a rhetorical ritual is a recurring act of formalized language or gesture that is both instrumental and mythic.[6] A rebirth ritual, a rhetorical enactment of myth, aims to transform identities. The Reagan film, as a rebirth ritual, attempted to create political and cultural identities that were tied to the Republican ideology. It exploited and perpetuated a renewed sense of material and spiritual well-being, while its images of metamorphosis appeared to resolve the ambiguities and contradictions on the surfaces of American life. The film both exemplified and set the tone for the campaign to come, as Ronald Reagan offered himself as the symbolic resolution of the problems and dilemmas that had plagued America until the purported new beginning.

The visual form and communicative techniques that differentiated the campaign film from traditional political discourse increased its ability to communicate on a mythic level. While a speaker at a podium has recourse to imagistic language to evoke myth, a film benefits from the perception that visual images reflect a reality that exists independently of a speaker. In the Reagan film, mythic visual images provided common points of orientation for an otherwise heterogeneous audience, thus increasing its efficacy as a transformative rhetorical ritual.

A New Beginning as Rebirth Ritual

Rebirth, implied by the film's title, *A New Beginning*, is one of the most prevalent kinds of rhetorical rituals. Rebirth rhetoric often accompanies periods of transition such as changes of political or social status.[7] The campaign film represented the point where the primary campaign ended and the 1984 presidential campaign began. Ronald Reagan was both president and candidate for president; through the film, he both recapitulated the past and heralded the future.

In a larger sense, not only the film but the entire sociopolitical context was transitional. Ronald Reagan's first term in office had initiated a break with liberal democratic policies of the past, but he had not yet completed his task, the construction of a conservative Republican government.

Rhetorical rebirth rituals are best able to achieve their aim, the transformation of identity, in the transitional period between political ideologies. Their mythic aspects are designed to transform identity by overcoming the contradictions and resolving the uncertainties that mark the transitional period. Further, American society consists of contradictory myths that help to rationalize behavior and provide models for action. Indeed, American history and politics can be construed as a struggle between dialectically opposing myths. Typically, one myth or aspect of the dialectic becomes dominant in order to explain social situations.[8] In transitional periods of social crisis or change, prevailing myths may become inadequate. As a result, shifts in value orientation are achieved through enactments—or rituals—of transformation. Politics, in particular, is a dramatic stage upon which value changes are expressed through myths. The myth of rebirth, enacted by symbolic conflict and resolution, helps to explain and justify social and political change.[9]

Metamorphosis is the metaphorical concept that structures rhetorical rituals of rebirth. In *A New Beginning*, many images imply conflict, separation, and sacrifice; these transform into positive images of unity, stability, and integration. Darkness, death, and the past are associated with conflict, suffering, and strife. However, because the film is a ritual of rebirth—positive transformation and integration—there are relatively few negative images. The film's emphasis is upon new-found unity, harmony, and consensus rather than upon conflict, which necessitates resolution. A detailed analysis of *A New Beginning* will reveal the specific ways in which the myth of rebirth was conveyed by verbal and visual means.

The first scene opens in darkness, at Reagan's 1980 Inaugural Address, which is itself a transitional event. The black screen, defined only by the date and the voice of Ronald Reagan taking his oath of office, marks both a separation from the past and the "new beginning" of the Reagan administration. The next image is a movement from dark to light; early morning sunlight fills the sky. In scene 2, Reagan verbally reinforces this connection by referring back to scene 1: "Yes, it was quite a day," he says, "a new beginning."

Upward movements also imply positive metamorphosis. In the first image of Ronald Reagan and George Bush together (scene 2), the camera pans vertically from their feet to their faces. This movement itself would not necessarily carry great import. However, in the context of the many other upward movements repeated throughout the film, introducing the Reagan-Bush team in this manner links them to America's positive transformation. Metamorphosis is suggested both verbally and visually. In scene 3, for instance, George Bush attributes America's rebirth to Ronald Reagan:

> It's just different. The mood is different. . . . The, the . . . it's not that everybody agrees with what you're doing, but there's a, there's a certain respect for the United States of America and it is loud, and it is clear, and I, I run into that all over the country. People say, "You know, we're pleased that the president is taking these strong positions," and they might argue with you on one or two things if you give 'em a chance, but they're back. You get the feeling that the country's moving again, a certain pride level.

Bush's comment sets the tone for the scenes to come, where ordinary Americans marvel at the renewed feeling of pride and patriotism (scene 4); people express their satisfaction with the economic recovery (scene 9); Lee Greenwood sings a patriotic song about America (scene 5); and Ronald Reagan celebrates the "reawakening" of military pride and patriotism (scene 6). Bush intimates in this scene that some people may not agree with Reagan administration policies. However, his remark is quickly overshadowed by a set of interviews with five Americans who enthusiastically endorse Bush's claim that America is "back." This group consists of men, women, blacks, whites, Hispanics, workers, and members of the middle class. They all agree that America has experienced a spiritual and/or economic revival that can be attributed to Ronald Reagan. There is no hint of dissent or disagreement. This minimizes the credibility of Bush's comments that "it's not that everybody agrees with what you're doing" and "there are people who might argue with you on one or two things." Rather, the unity and consensus of this diverse group of Americans seems to indicate widespread popular support for the Reagan administration.

America's "rebirth" is conveyed by the visual use of the flag. The traditional symbol of "freedom," and thus, of the renewed feeling of pride and patriotism, is continually waved, raised, and saluted. It appears in a total of twenty-eight shots during the film. The flag often appears alongside children, who connote innocence and the future. In scene 1, for instance, a long-shot of a flag being hoisted is followed by a close-up of a child's face as she gazes up at it. Again, in scene 5, a music video montage, three images of children are shown alongside the flag when the song lyrics say "freedom" or "free." In one shot sequence, an extreme close-up of a billowing flag with its edges extending beyond the film frame makes it appear to be larger than life, rather than an object presented from the perspective of the human eye (as realist or traditional documentary images would be shown). This is followed by an image of a young boy saluting the same flag. Only its corner appears in the lower right-hand side of the frame, but its lines and dimensions are consistent with those of the first image. In this way, the flag is presented as the dominant, all-encompassing symbol of America; its boundaries extend out to reach the American people. The young boy's salute is not only a military gesture, implicitly suggesting the need to defend the flag, but it is also a sign of welcome and well-being. Symbolically, the child represents America's rebirth, its return to innocence. This shot is followed by one of the Statue of Liberty encased in scaffolding, a subtle reminder that America's ideal of freedom has been threatened in the past, just as it is a practical example of the urban and institutional decay that the Reagan administration would alleviate. The statue is, thus, being rebuilt; the flag is raised and respected anew. These images are accompanied by the song lyrics, "The flag still stands for freedom, and they can't take that away." This section closes with a firmly centered image of the White House with the flag flying high in front. The White House, a metonymy for America, connotes the stability and unity available to all Americans as they rally round the banner of "freedom."

Both the White House and the flag are presented as coterminous with Ronald Reagan as well as with America. Scene 2 opens with a backlit image of the White House which, as a result, appears to glow softly in the early morning sun. Images of the White House dissolve into that of Ronald Reagan, also backlit, seated at his desk. In contrast to the more disjunctive cuts, which are typically used to make transitions between shots, dissolves used in such a fashion indicate unity and relatedness. Through this use of visual conventions, Ronald Reagan (and his administration) become inseparable from the White House, just as the White House represents both Ronald Reagan and America. Thus, in this scene and the sequence it introduces, Reagan is depicted as a leader who is in control; at the same time, cooperation and camaraderie within the White House ranks are emphasized—all without benefit of verbal language.

Even when conflict is acknowledged, it is done so with great subtlety and then quickly dismissed. Reagan asserts that as president he is exposed to opposition as well as agreement. As he speaks, a still photograph of Ronald Reagan and Tip O'Neill, then the liberal democratic Speaker of the House and Reagan's most vociferous political opponent, flashes onscreen. The short duration of the shot minimizes its impact. The shot is so brief that the image is barely recognizable. Far more memorable, because lengthier and more numerous, are the preceding and following shots which show Reagan surrounded by his cooperative political allies. Still photographs depict him conversing with several members of his cabinet, after which he participates at a cabinet meeting. Everyone is alert and smiling; in one shot, two men whisper together. As these images pass by, Reagan lauds the men and women who have sacrificed their private lives for public service. All in all, the internal mechanisms of the White House appear to run smoothly. Like America itself, the White House is characterized by unity, harmony, and consensus.

Scene 5 briefly depicts the coffin of a dead soldier, perhaps a casualty from Lebanon. An image of integration follows as a live soldier is hugged by a woman. The song lyrics that underscore the first image are "I won't forget the men who died"; for the second, "Who gave that right [freedom] to me." This latter image also contains a gun, a baby, and a flag, which links patriotism to a strong defense and the protection of America's future. Not surprisingly, this image is followed by one of a flag being hoisted. There is a shift from separation to integration, achieved through the rebirth of American pride and patriotism. This is implicitly, but pragmatically, linked to military strength.

Images of positive metamorphosis are most apparent in scene 8, where Reagan celebrates economic renewal. Here, the transition from the liberal past, full of sacrifice, suffering, and despair, to the positive present is suggested through a stream of newspaper headlines that progress from bad news (during the Carter Administration) to good news (after Reagan takes office). These "factual" images are surrounded by those of people building, making, and buying (themselves images of metamorphosis), as Reagan reasserts that his administration has overcome the reified "evil" of inflation and has made it possible for people to prosper again.[10]

Additionally, in scene 10, where Reagan appeals to the elderly, on two separate occasions an older couple walk hand in hand down the street, and their paths are crossed by children. The past meets the future. In one of the few dark images that appear in the film, two elderly people stroll along a beach and are silhouetted in the sunset. Reagan refers to them in the past tense; he will keep his promise to those who "kept" their promise to society. As with the "men who died," they are not to be forgotten. America can be reborn only through the hard work and sacrifices made in the past; out of the old arises the new.

Regeneration is further reinforced in the D-Day sequence (scene 13), which is basically a filmed rite of purification.[11] This most emotionally powerful scene of the film implicitly defends Reagan's militarism by relating America's war-torn past to its future glory. The surviving war heroes from D-Day are commemorated. Reagan takes note of the "ordinary heroes" who made America great. "Where do we find such men?" he ponders.[12] He quotes General Marshall, who had referred to them as "the best damn kids in the world." As he speaks, the camera pans the now-aged faces; it lingers as one man wipes away a tear. Lisa Zanatta Henn sobs as Reagan reads the letter she has written in honor of her father. His voice chokes with emotion, accentuating the dramatic intensity of the occasion. He strolls through the graveyard with Nancy Reagan, their figures small amidst the rows of crosses that overwhelm the screen. Nancy lays a wreath at the grave of Theodore Roosevelt, Jr., while solemn music plays in the background. This is the remembered past, where noble men unquestioningly sacrificed their lives for righteous causes. It is not the past of Vietnam, or even Lebanon or Grenada. Its "reality" is reinforced by grainy, black-and-white archival footage of the troops landing in Normandy, accompanied by spates of gunfire on the soundtrack. The past is selectively recalled, but only to confirm that it has been transcended by the "new beginning" made possible by the Reagan Administration. The new beginning is represented by Ronald Reagan who unifies fact and fiction, past and present, young and old. Reagan closes this scene with a thinly veiled plea for a military build-up, "We will always be prepared so we may be always free."

Reagan's trips to Japan, Korea, and China (scene 12) and his final exhortation for peace (Scene 15) are important elements of this rhetorical ritual of rebirth. His trip symbolizes the meeting of the opposing cultures of East and West. The prototype for this is the American frontier, which was the historical meeting-point for the "civilized" East and the Western wilderness. It later became America's self-proclaimed responsibility to extend the frontiers of freedom not only to its Western borders, but throughout the world. In this context Reagan posits a "new frontier," as he states, "Our trip to Japan, Korea, and later the People's Republic of China makes you realize that the old line "Go West, young man, go West" still fits. There's a new frontier out there, there's a future, and the United States is going to be very much a part of that future."

Reagan's statement takes on a deeper import when considered along with the visual imagery it accompanies. His words are synchronized with a shot of Japanese people waving Japanese and American flags together. This is followed by a shot where American flags predominate. Despite the threat of increasing Japanese dominance in the world economy, Reagan implicitly reassures Americans that their country will continue to be superior.

He also patronizes the Japanese, Koreans, and Chinese by referring to them as "they" although Americans are "we." "One cannot meet with those people," he says, "without realizing that they are a tremendously capable people, a talented and energetic people, and I found that there was a great longing for peace among those people." By choosing this language, Reagan exploits the perceived otherness of the East to unify Americans around a common "we," and he implies that there are significant differences between these countries and America. He seems to suggest that Americans naturally want peace, but it is less certain that citizens of other countries do as well. Visually, the opposition between Reagan and the Chinese premier is indicated by a still photograph that shows the two men standing across a table, separated by a white line of papers that run vertically down the center of the frame. Their handshake extends across this "barrier," implying reconciliation, the union of opposites.

Reagan could have stressed similarities rather than differences. Japan and South Korea were already capitalist countries and American allies. Reagan's trip to Communist China was a show of support for a country that had recently announced new policies of free enterprise and cultural exchange. In a nonthreatening and non-explicit way, the scene indicated that Reagan was committed to peace, albeit with American allies, and that he would talk to Communists, albeit those who lean towards capitalism.

Peace is an extremely important theme in *A New Beginning*, although, like freedom and liberty, it is never defined. In scene 15, Reagan directly addresses the American people with a final affirmation of his commitment to peace.[13] Visually, the viewer is taken on a tour from the Oval Office to the Roosevelt Room; verbally, the viewer is taken on a tour through American history. The camera lingers upon a series of Reagan's family photographs, but then moves forward (and back) onto images of American tradition and history. To further develop this nostalgic mood, Reagan asserts, "You can't help but choke up a little bit because you're surrounded by history that somehow has touched everything in this room . . . and it occurs to you that everyone who has ever sat here yearned in the depths of his soul to bring Americans together in peace." As he speaks, the screen is occupied by a set of miniature soldiers from the World War II battle of Bastogne, a gift given to the president during his trip to Normandy. Here, not only are years of complicated history collapsed into a few brief images, but Reagan glosses over a contradiction: peace gained through war.

When the camera pans to the Roosevelt Room, Reagan reminds the viewers that this room is named for both presidents named Roosevelt: "one a Democrat and one a Republican." He makes no other references to the Democrats by name throughout the film, but this reference at a moment when peace and conciliation are being stressed is typical of the careful orchestration of the entire film. Reagan makes only vague allusions to America prior to his 1980 election. Throughout the film, real controversy is elided. Reagan's comment that one room could be named for presidents of different parties minimizes their differences. It implies that party disagreements can be reconciled, that both Democrats and Republicans share the same ideals. This also furthers the Republican aim of winning the traditionally Democratic vote. The subtle message intimates that the parties are not that far apart, so why not vote Republican?

Overall, consensus and resolution of conflict is the message conveyed by *A New Beginning*. For this reason, neither the Democrats nor the Soviet Union—Reagan's adversaries at the time—is given much screen time, even though the Democrats were challenging him for the presidency and he viewed the Soviet Union as America's ideological opposite. Here, as in 1980, Reagan emerges as a man of peace by avoiding explicit reference to the Soviet Union. The threat of a foreign enemy is only implied, as, for example, when Reagan visits the military, refers to "the frontiers of freedom," or celebrates American war heroes. Just before Reagan's final direct address to the viewing audience, the camera pans slowly to the five service flags, and to the streamers that represent every American war and battle fought since the Revolutionary War. Shot in close-up, Reagan sits at his desk and concludes, "My fondest hope for this presidency is that the people give us the continued opportunity to pursue a peace so lasting and so strong that we'd never have to add another streamer to those flags." His remark is yet another plug for stronger military defense in "pursuit" of peace. Throughout the film, the preponderance of military imagery and reminders of World War II justify Reagan's belief, realized in actual defense spending, that military strength would maintain peace. America may have been "reborn," but it is a rebirth that must be guarded and protected.

Crucially, in this "America reborn," Reagan himself personifies the reawakening of the positive national identity; he is America's idealized image of itself. If rhetorical rituals are to be effective, subjective transformation must be enacted. Reagan himself had to embody America's new beginning. His own transformation and subsequent rebirth was enacted in scene 11, which replayed footage from the assassination attempt, which occurred on 30 March 1981. The symbolic import of this event did not go unnoticed. Not only did presidential biographer Lou Cannon claim that this turned Reagan into a "mythic" figure,[14] but *Village Voice* reporter Mark Hertsgaard wrote that the assassination attempt gave the Reagan Administration "a new life. . . . It had new symbolic capital."[15] Afterward, it was as if Reagan's recovery mirrored America's own process of renewal. Both had, in a sense, symbolically died and had been reborn in a more positive incarnation.

The myth of rebirth served the interests of the Reagan administration and conservative upper-class Americans more so than other groups. It appeared, on the surface, to suggest metamorphosis and integration. This was accomplished by excluding terms, events, and interpretations that could not be accommodated and that did not suit the Republicans' purposes. Ronald Reagan's myth of a new beginning was both "true" and illusory; it functioned as a unifying social bond that articulated a reality for those who subscribed to it. At the same time, from the more distanced perspective of the critic on the outside of the myth, "a new beginning" was a mirage that benefited the few at the expense of the many.

5 Rebirth of Myth in *A New Beginning*

> *Myths are the mechanisms by which people believe contradicto-
> ry things simultaneously; they are also the mechanism by which
> those contradictions are (as people believe) resolved—or at least
> held in a tension which is not uncomfortable to the believers.*
> —*James Oliver Robertson,*
> American Myth, American Reality

Rebirth of Myth

The myth of rebirth was an interpretive frame that attained the practical purpose of gaining support, in the form of votes, for Ronald
Reagan's conservative ideology. The Republican use of this myth
demonstrated how myths can serve instrumental purposes, in this
case the election of a president. Yet the positive, reassuring myth of
rebirth was not all that was used to gain adherence to the conservative agenda. Another way of framing *A New Beginning* is to examine
the particular myths that appear in the film in relation to social and
historical exigencies. This interpretive frame suggests that the
Republicans celebrated the rebirth of myth itself in the historical context of the Reagan presidency.

Beginning in the 1960s and throughout the 1970s, many
American myths, in all of their dialectically opposing manifestations,
were challenged and contested. There was a crisis in the values that
together made up the American mythos. Thus, it was not enough
simply to emphasize one myth or one set of values. Rather, as
Reagan and his advisers seemed to have intuitively realized, it was
more efficacious to enact a reaffirmation of the contradictory myths
that defined and delimited American beliefs, values, and attitudes.[1]
Reagan's rhetoric managed to affirm and regenerate contradictory
myths through the transformative rhetoric and mythic imagery of
rebirth.

Like most myths, the images and words that constructed *A New Beginning* offered solace, certitude, and explanations of the world. However, instead of stressing one set of opposing myths over another, Reagan emphasized both. The myths he invoked provided unity through a dialectical reaffirmation of opposites, such as those that mark the tension between subjective and objective, private and public, individual and community. Throughout the film, seemingly contradictory American myths—materialism or moralism, the primacy of the individual or the community; or the president as leader or as man of the people—were reconciled and revitalized.

A *New Beginning* appeared to reaffirm simultaneously both sides of opposing myths. This helped the Republicans to effect personal and political transformation in accord with their conservative ideology. Throughout the film, Ronald Reagan and American citizens pointed to economic revitalization and a reawakening of pride, optimism, and patriotism across the land. This overriding vision of rebirth was related to basic, familiar myths that defined American identity and beliefs, as well as the policies of the Reagan administration: the myths of the American Dream, the individual versus the community, and the president. In consequence, the image of a cohesive "new beginning" appeared to coincide with Reagan's political programs, and the social order was maintained by transforming perceptions of it.

Myth of the American Dream

One of America's most fundamental myths is expressed in what has often been termed America's civil religion, the myth of the American Dream, which is related to the myth of rebirth. From its origins, America has been conceived as the New World, a land of liberty, equality, and opportunity, where both individuals and society as a whole would prosper. To its largely immigrant population, America was often conceived as a second chance, a place where one could start anew.

There are, however, two dichotomous versions of the myth of the American Dream—the materialistic and the moralistic—that reflect different notions of America's nature and purpose.[2] Throughout American history, political candidates have typically aligned themselves with one or the other versions of this myth in order to interpret the present, to relate their policies to American ideals, and to forge a unified national identity. Both versions of the myth of the American Dream express the values of the Protestant work ethic out of which capitalism emerged, although their differences reflect the historical division between the Republican and Democratic parties. The materialistic myth is associated with the traditional Republican position. It emphasizes individual initiative as the means to happiness and prosperity; it presupposes the value of competition, free enterprise, and individual freedom from governmental regulation and restraint. It promises that hard work will be rewarded, and presumes that individuals act on the basis of self-interest rather than concern for the social good. The moralistic myth, more characteristic of the Democratic view, emphasizes a need for community and society that may supersede individual needs; it is based upon a belief in equality, rights to liberty and pursuit of happiness, and the values of tolerance, charity, and compassion.

Throughout the twentieth century, American society became increasingly distant from the agrarian, small-town, Protestant ethic that had preceded industrialization. By the 1970s, marked by a general crisis in beliefs and values, both materialistic and moralistic versions of the American Dream had become debilitated. The materialistic myth, which had dominated early free-market capitalism, fostered self-interested individualism at the expense of social needs and values. The individual who sought prosperity necessarily competed with others who desired the same, and efforts to enjoy the benefits of society prevented others from doing so. Emphasis upon material prosperity unrelated to virtue severed the individual from any moral ethic.[3] The moralistic myth, its ascendance coincident with the rise of liberalism, stressed the values of equality, cooperation, and compassion, but only insofar as they facilitated productivity. With liberalism, social goals and values became increasingly determined by technological goals, most notably economic growth and profits. As the autonomous individual was deemphasized, individual fulfillment became increasingly dependent upon products, goods, and services provided by the technostructure. Happiness became equated with consumption rather than production. The values expressed by the moralistic myth, too, became increasingly inapplicable to the modern world. Capitalism was guided by no ethic, and thus its myths lost their power.

Ronald Reagan's "rebirth" appeared to revitalize both the materialistic and moralistic versions of the American Dream. His program was characterized as Jeffersonian Republicanism, itself a union of opposites that coincided to a large extent with the materialistic/moralistic dichotomy. While Reagan's policies promoted a return to the self-regulating free-market economy and the values that sustained it, in fact he retained the liberal values of economic and technological growth as the means to produce the good life. His strategy indicated the inherent morality of the American people because of their materialism—materialism being characterized as the ability to produce and consume. He addressed this contradiction by stressing the shared values of equality, family, and community (the moralistic values of the public domain) through which individual virtues, such as independence, initiative, and enterprise, could be rewarded.

In *A New Beginning*, while production remains a virtue in the public realm of work, consumption remains a virtue in the private sphere. Thus, images of growth and prosperity, which reconcile production and consumption, permeate the film. Scenes 5 and 8 repeatedly show houses and buildings under construction. In scene 5 a family moves out of a house, only to reappear in scene 8 as they move into a more spacious abode. Reagan claims that Americans are once again able to purchase homes and cars, and his words are illustrated by this same family, who also have a shiny new truck parked in the driveway. The family owns a new truck rather than luxury car; the implicit claim is that Reagan's policies benefit the working classes. Both the new home and truck symbolize the materialistic side of the American Dream: to own a progressively larger single-family home, to be socially and physically mobile, to possess property. These two symbols, which celebrate the economic recovery, provide a clear expression of the materialistic myth and underline Reagan's appeal to the majority.

Other images in the film celebrate the fact that people are able to consume again. "People are spending more, traveling more, going on vacations," marvels one woman (scene 9). Her comment highlights the moralistic myth, with its emphasis upon equality, liberty, and the pursuit of happiness. Everyone is prosperous in Ronald Reagan's America. In scene 8 a man weighs a huge fish, and a waitress takes an order at a diner. Prosperity demonstrated by increased consumption is also implied by all of the lush farm images scattered throughout the film. Produce is either growing or being harvested. There is production, and this necessitates consumption.[4]

Consumption is, however, identified with the virtuous principles upon which the moralistic myth of the social order is founded; it is also associated with the principles of individual freedom, initiative, and enterprise that define the materialistic myth.

The Place of the Individual Versus the Nature of Community

Closely related to the myth of the American Dream are those myths that deal with the contradiction between the individual and community. This contradiction is best articulated by the western myth, one of America's central myths. Will Wright, in *Sixguns and Society*, points out that in a market society, the rugged, autonomous, and independent individual is opposed to the weak and dependent society (or community). In contrast, with the liberal planned economy, individualism is deemphasized; the individual is dependent on the strong society.[5]

The personal and political crises of the sixties and seventies indicated that the values of both individualism and community had become debilitated; prior to the "new beginning," America's myths were becoming untenable. However, the images of the Reagan film strengthened both the myth of the individual and the community. Reagan stressed both individual initiative and traditional community values as the means to a strong America. Both the independent individual and the strong, communal society are regenerated in *A New Beginning*. Family and neighborhood, rather than government or organizations, provide a homogenous set of values that guide and define social relations. The individual is part of these groups, but most important, is independent from the paternalistic government. The rugged individual is free to strive, to attain, to become a producer rather than a consumer of the benefits of society.

In order to convey this conception of the individual/community dichotomy, *A New Beginning* harkens back to the myth of the West. Throughout American history, the peculiarly American character has been defined by this myth. In fact, Frederick Jackson Turner's famous "Frontier Thesis" attributes the American character, as symbolized by the frontiersman, to contact with the wilderness. Turner names several resultant qualities of the quintessential "American": cooperation, optimism, individualism, self-reliance, resiliency, steadfastness, neighborliness, confidence, wholesomeness, enthusiasm, calmness of purpose, spirit of adventure, and initiative.[6]

Ronald Carpenter notes that although this thesis could be, and was, used to support either the materialistic or moralistic version of the American Dream, or to support either individualism or the need for community, it has remained the rhetorical source of the American identity.[7] Historically, it was expressed through the pioneer, the yeoman farmer, and later, the cowboy. Indeed, A New Beginning is populated with images of the cowboy. Many of the ordinary Americans who appear are dressed in western style. Even Ronald Reagan appears in scene 14 riding his horse on his ranch in California. Virtually all of the men (apart from those who are interviewed on the street) and Reagan when he is not being "president," are dressed in red-and-white checkered shirts. In scenes 1 and 5, men are even wearing cowboy hats. In scene 1, a "cowboy" stands in a corral, with lasso in hand, as horses pass calmly in front of him. The "wild" horses have been tamed. A shot follows of a construction worker pointing upward as he directs a crane. Like the cowboy who has tamed the horse, he has controlled the machine. Similarly, the various construction workers and laborers who appear in the film are the new "urban cowboys." Like their forebears, these men are smiling, optimistic, and symbolically bathed in sunshine as they perform their day's work.

What differentiates the cowboy from other mythic images such as the pioneer or the yeoman farmer is that the cowboy is an employee.[8] The cowboy, while a rugged individual, works for someone else. He remains an individual, but is dependent upon someone else for his livelihood. The latter-day cowboy is a professional who works for profit rather than any particular set of values.[9]

Reagan's cowboy works both for individual profit and for the values defined by community. For instance, the song "God Bless the USA" begins: "If tomorrow all the things were gone I'd worked for all my life." The images that articulate this show a young child hugging a figure who presumably is her father, a traditional wedding, and a house being built, stressing the importance of family rather than economic success for its own sake.

Throughout A New Beginning, the myth of community is reaffirmed through its characterization of a small-town America that consists of unified groups of nuclear families and neighborhoods. It is in this monolithic vision of a society composed of shared values that the individual finds a place. Individuals in the film do not strive to become members of organizations, to get promotions in a corporation, or to become part of the technostructure as a measure of their success. In fact, there are few images of industrial America. There is a token cityscape presented in scene 5, and a few workers are interviewed against a metropolitan background. Needless to say, none of the homeless who crowd the city streets appear in the film.

For the most part, the film consists of nostalgic images of the small town. Yet the rural, small-town community does not reflect the experience of most Americans, who live in urban, or suburban, environments. This myth of the small-town community has three important functions: it makes it possible to emphasize individualism (because there is a simultaneous belief in social conformity); it demonstrates the democratic nature of American society (which, because there is unity and consensus of values, is the expression of the collective will of the people); and it provides a secure sense of unchanging rootedness in a society that is increasingly changing and uprooted.[10] By the mid-1970s, many Americans felt that they had lost the values of shared community life. Thus, the Reagan film revitalized this myth of community by presenting images of small-town America in the context of present-day realities, while simultaneously supporting the myth of individualism.

The myth of community is evoked early on in *A New Beginning*. In scene 1, a paperboy on his bicycle rides down a tree-lined avenue. A briefcase-toting man crosses the sidewalk in front of him and calls "Good morning, Jim," as he steps into a car where another man and woman wait. The exchange, like the depiction of a car pool, conveys a sense of community. People here know each other's names; the anonymity associated with the city does not exist. People smile and wave; throughout the film, people are together, whether at an outdoor picnic, a political rally, or as they meander down the street eating ice cream.

Further, rural America is disproportionately represented. The film opens with a single plow moving across a field although the number of small farms still operating in America was steadily diminishing at the time. The next image, too, shows a farmhouse where a small truck moves out of frame and a rooster crows to indicate morning. Again, this idyllic image of rural America is familiar to the vast majority of Americans—from movies rather than experience.

A New Beginning celebrated both individualism and community as vital forces in the America represented by Ronald Reagan. His particular blend of these two myths aligned him with populism. Like the traditional populist movement in America, he was opposed to bureaucracy and the forces of organization. Although his policies were consistently criticized because they favored corporate America rather than the individual or family, he elided this problem by keeping corporate America out of the film. Just as the film shunned any direct reference to the Soviet Union, Central America, or the Middle East in describing Reagan's foreign policy, so the deleterious effects of urbanization and technology did not impinge on the film's representation of the myths of the individual and community. *A New Beginning* presented a myth undisturbed by reality.

Myth of the President

Most important, Reagan successfully revitalized and redefined the myth of the president in *A New Beginning*. The myth of the president has always been the focal point for American myths concerning power and how it should be wielded. As the symbolic representative of the American people, the president embodies, and thus mediates, the contradictory values expressed in the dichotomous myths of the American Dream and the individual versus the community. Reagan's ability to mediate contradictions as a means to transform values enabled him to forge a renewed sense of national identity.

Walter Fisher writes in "Rhetorical FIction and the Presidency" that as the symbolic representative of the American people, the president has persuasive force in defining the nature of persons, community, and the nation.[11] Presidents' conceptions of their relationships with the people reveal their images of themselves and their roles. Typically, presidents take on the roles of leaders or men of the people. Reagan is presented as both in *A New Beginning*. As a "man of the people," Reagan emphasizes the moralistic myth of the American Dream and the values of community that are associated with the Democratic vision. As did and do preeminent Democrats like Franklin Delano Roosevelt and Ted Kennedy, Reagan appeals to the "common people" and the values that have traditionally united them. For example, Fisher quotes Kennedy who defines the Democratic cause in the following passage: "Our commitment has been, since the days of Thomas Jefferson, to all those he called the 'humble members' of society—the farmers, mechanics, and laborers. . . . On this foundation we have defined our values, refined our policies, and refreshed our faith."[12]

Ronald Reagan could comfortably have made this same claim in *A New Beginning*. Part of Reagan's populist appeal was aimed at gaining traditionally Democrat voting blocs, among them farmers, workers, the young and the elderly. Images of these groups populate the film, to the exclusion of great urban industrial centers, bureaucrats, technocrats, the indigenous or the elite. None of these were meant to be part of Ronald Reagan's America. Unlike Nixon, Reagan did not appear to be an elite leader divorced from the needs and interests of the majority; nor, like Presidents Ford and Carter, was he so much a man of the people that his leadership abilities were questioned. Rather, he straddled both positions. By appealing to the independent individual in the name of the community, and by appearing to unite both the materialistic and moralistic versions of the American Dream, Reagan also reaffirmed the myth of the president as both hero and man of the people, a myth endemic to American populism.

In accord with the myth of rebirth, the prototype for the populist myth of the president is Christ.[13] Like Christ, and mythologized American heroes such as George Washington, Thomas Jefferson, and Abraham Lincoln, Reagan is presented as a heroic savior who will redeem "the people." As mythic figures, presidential "heroes" embody contradictions and provide the means to overcome them. In order to do so, they must fulfill certain criteria: the hero must be of obscure and mysterious origins (exemplified by the log-cabin myth in American political mythology); he embarks upon a quest and encounters evil, suffering, or death; he overcomes this challenge and is purified or transformed. In this way, mythic heroes can be redeemers, as Reagan appeared to be in *A New Beginning*.[14]

Even a cursory glance at *A New Beginning* reveals that Reagan located himself in this myth of the presidential hero. Throughout the film, he alluded to his common origins in order to unite himself with the American people whom he represented, defined as the political center, the middle-class majority. This enabled Reagan to allay criticisms that he was a rich man's president, whose policies favored corporate America and the elite, without having to refute the charges actively.

When Reagan appeals to the elderly in scene 10, he begins by claiming that he is a senior citizen himself. Here, he stares directly into the camera, and it closes in upon his face, which is marked by lines and wrinkles. He dresses in casual attire—the checkered shirt—and his on-camera appeal follows two interviews with elderly people who are filmed in a similar fashion. He is presented here in a way that makes him almost indistinguishable from them; it is probably not incidental that this scene is followed by the depiction of the assassination attempt upon his life. This event elevated him to divine status; he confronted death, overcame the challenge, and became imbued with the power to lead.

Reagan is quick to point out that he is merely the instrument of the people's will. He has been called to serve them. In scene 2, he remarks, "You don't really become president. The presidency is an institution, and you have temporary custody of it." However, while he denies that he is an "elite" leader, removed from a community of peers, the images and symbols that surround him speak otherwise. He denies that he has a lonely job where he must make decisions as an individual. However, as he speaks the camera shows him working diligently—and alone—at his desk. A placard on his desk reads "It can be done" and a navigator's compass sits beside it. Even when he is later shown surrounded by his helpers (necessary for any "hero") he is assigned greater status by being allocated more space. He is not simply one of them.

Towards the end of the film (scene 14) Reagan is seen relaxing at home on his ranch. Here he embodies the typical American. He wears a T-shirt and is shown working in the yard. He states that he enjoys "the simple things—riding horses, chopping wood, spending time with Nancy, being outdoors, and close to all of God's natural gifts." (The image that accompanies his words shows him using a jigsaw rather than chopping wood; there are also two men helping him with his task). But for the most part, he epitomizes the rugged individual of the American West in both words and imagery. As the scene opens, he is shown riding his horse in the distance, an echo of director John Ford's western motifs. All of Ford's westerns deal with the contradiction between the individual and society, and in the end celebrate the rugged individual. Reagan differs from this myth only in that Nancy is always at his side. She serves, however, primarily to confirm his rugged individualism. She knows her place. She smiles and gazes up at her husband as he performs his "presidential" duties.

Throughout *A New Beginning*, visual techniques assist Reagan in mediating the contradictions implicit in the requirement that a presidential hero be both a leader and a man of the people. In scene 1, the image of Ronald Reagan taking his oath of office is intercut with images of America and Americans. These dissolve into one another, but are separated from shots of Ronald Reagan by cuts. The direction of movement in each frame is always oriented toward Ronald Reagan, a centered image of stasis amidst the movement that is

America. Additionally, the images of Ronald Reagan's inauguration depict an "actual" historic event that has more weight than the obviously fictional images of the American people. Although he is among the people, he stands out as their leader.

During the scenes where Reagan directly addresses the audience, his mediation of the contradiction between being a leader and a man of the people, an individual and part of a community, is also expressed through visual means. Scene 15 is a case in point. Like all mythic heroes, Reagan has a goal, which he articulates here: to ensure a strong and lasting peace. He is in center-frame, and there are no distracting background objects to divert attention from him. The background here is much less cluttered than in the shots of many of the other "ordinary Americans" who are interviewed, which assigns more status to Ronald Reagan. The camera closes in on his face, the extreme close-up making him appear to be larger than life. The shot confers authority on him and elevates him in his role as leader. The use of still photographs throughout the film also serves this function. First used by Nixon media consultant Gene Wyckoff in 1960, Wyckoff later observed that this technique was "extraordinarily suitable for conveying an impression of an heroic image, perhaps because each still photograph in itself is a slightly unreal impression, a moment frozen from life, that makes it easier for viewers to accept and be moved by an illusion of the candidate's heroic dimension."[15]

Yet, at the same time that Reagan is presented as a hero, the very closeness and intimacy of the television images help to create the impression that he is one of the people. His soothing tones, his attire, and even the extreme close-ups that focus upon his twinkling blue eyes: all create the appearance of accessibility. He speaks to the people, he is one of them, and thus he is responsive to their needs and interests.

A New Beginning was not designed to persuade its audience through discursive arguments. On the contrary, the Republicans relied heavily upon television's capacity to communicate myths through which implicit political discourse could be understood. Myths were evoked to recreate a unified and cohesive American identity. From the perspective of the reader on the "inside" of the myths, he offered and represented a genuine reaffirmation of contradictory myths, subsumed under the overriding myth of rebirth. In consequence, a political rhetorical ritual became indistinguishable from a social, mythic ritual, and the "rebirth" that the Republicans proclaimed was as much a rhetorical renewal of myth as a mythic representation of reality. The problem was that, from a more critical perspective, the resultant combination of myth and theory that formed the Republican ideology was inadequate as a means to cope with a complex reality.

6 The Artful Use of Visual Cliché

At the same time that oral discourse becomes transformed into an archaic ritual and increasingly drained of its linguistic content by electronic media, oratory revives pre-literate modes of expression to articulate a rigidly defined and narrow ground of discourse. While this transformed rhetorical display appears to some as irrelevant, trite, and cliché-ridden grandiloquence, it is also clear that it is a form of oral communication which survives precisely because of its reliance upon simplicity, a familiar stock of received "wisdom," and the invocation of accepted commonplaces. . . . Rhetorical commonplace and stylization are the strengths rather than the flaws of political oratory. . . . Persuasion, conflict or the disposition of specialized information play virtually no part in such an oratory.
—Paul Cocoran, Political Language and Rhetoric

A New Beginning coordinated mythic images from different discursive genres. These images were united to convey one coherent myth of rebirth, a strategy that enhanced the perceived "reality" of the film despite its quite obvious excursions into fancy. In addition, the film revitalized particular American myths and in so doing, appeared to overcome contradictions. However, a final frame that explores the artful use of visual cliché is necessary to articulate the relation between mythic televisual images and political discourse.

Television is the primary purveyor of myth in contemporary American culture. Its images present, accumulate, and elaborate upon the common understandings that form and sustain the social foundation. The medium itself is a vehicle for what Michael Osborn calls *rhetorical depiction*, the master term of modern rhetoric.[1] According to Osborn, rhetorical depictions are simple mythic pictures that embody common values and goals. They join great masses of people together in megacommunities; their persuasive power emanates from their ability to "possess an audience at the moment of perceptual encounter," that is, to imprint themselves on consciousness prior to processes of reflection and analysis.

A New Beginning strategically recycled familiar and reassuring myths in order to reaffirm the bonds uniting Americans. The film was an artful assemblage of depictions that may be characterized as visual clichés. Cliché is used here in accordance with Anton Zijderveld's definition:

> A cliché is a traditional form of human expression (words, thoughts, emotions, gestures, acts) which—due to repetitive use in social life—has lost its original, often ingenuous, heuristic power. Although it thus fails positively to contribute meaning to social interactions and communication, it does function socially, since it manages to stimulate behavior (cognition, emotion, volition, action) while it avoids reflections on meaning.[2]

While Osborn's rhetorical depictions contribute positive meaning to social interactions, visual clichés are depictions that have lost substantive meaning; they function only to provoke an "emotional reflex" in the audience. Zijderveld argues that modern society is "clichogenic:" clichés function as mini-institutions because they represent traditional and collective forms of thinking, feeling, and acting. Clichés offer individuals stability and provide society with a recalcitrance that transcends individual actions. In this way, the very banality of these clichés, their simplicity and repetitiveness, renders them all the more persuasive as mythic visual forms. Clichés eliminate the need for reflection and the relativization of meaning that is an inevitable consequence of reflection. In an uncertain and ambiguous world, clichés help to maintain the appearance of stability and certainty.

In *A New Beginning*, visual clichés created a positive psychological image of Ronald Reagan and the America he represented. Clichés such as the flag, Air Force One, the Statue of Liberty, the space shuttle lifting off, even the American Olympic team, provoked an emotional, prereflective reaction. They had a unifying power; they articulated America's "rebirth" and helped Reagan to secure the allegiance of working- and middle-class Americans who made up the political majority.

The Republicans appeared to have recognized that in order to shift political alliances and create long-term conservative frames of mind, Reagan needed to reach the people on a personal as well as political level. The Republicans were also aware of the basic political fact that most voters, if not apathetic, had less than an in-depth relationship to politics. Roughly half (53.3 percent) of the eligible voters went to the polls in 1984; this did not differ significantly from 1980 (52.6 percent). But even this modest increase was the first in American presidential politics since 1960.

The Republicans needed to appeal to a lethargic populace. Thus, the political center they sought to win over was best reached through suggestive, emotional clichés rather than overtly "political" appeals. And what better medium than television with which to do so? A seminal study conducted by Herbert E. Krugman in 1969 found that thirty seconds after watching television, viewers' beta waves, indicative of alert, conscious attention, switched to alpha waves, characteristic of an unfocused, receptive lack of attention much like daydreaming. Further research revealed that the left hemisphere of the brain, which processes information analytically and logically, becomes inactive when a viewer is watching television, which allows the right hemisphere to process information emotionally and noncritically.[3] Thus, Krugman's study supports the notion that television images are processed more by an oral logic than by the analytical, formal logic characteristic of print media. John Fiske and John Hartley write that in contrast to formal logic, the oral logic of televisual communication is "validated by its context, by the opposition of elements (often visual/verbal), and not by the deductive requirements of the syllogism."[4]

A New Beginning's persuasive force was intensified by the Republicans' artful use of visual clichés, a strategy that took full advantage of the way television worked as a televisual communication form. The film's poetic organization used the oral logic of television to place familiar, clichéd images in a new context, and in so doing, provided a positive means with which to interpret present-day realities.

The Poetic-Image Mosaic of *A New Beginning*

A New Beginning was an admixture of visual clichés and conventions that together served to convince the viewer that things were better in America since Ronald Reagan had become president, that there had been both an economic and "spiritual" recovery. After the tumultuous sixties and seventies, viewers were constantly reminded

"America is back"; that is, the mythic America of nostalgic memory. At the same time, this message helped to redefine America's self-image, its people's conceptions of who they were and what they stood for. The combinations of familiar words, sounds, and images offered Americans positive images (both visual and psychological) of their president, their country, and themselves.

Although clearly not a traditional form of public address, the film did, like other discursive forms, put forth assertions meant to be accepted by an audience. In contrast to traditional rhetorical argument, however, the tools used were juxtapositions of words, images, shots, and scenes rather than oratory alone. The preedited and prearranged sequences of events left far less to chance than any "live" oratory could. The film was organized as poetic-image mosaic.[5]

Narrative (fiction), expository (documentary and news), and poetic (experimental film) are the three structuring principles of film that can be extrapolated to television.[6] Although they often overlap (as in the case of *A New Beginning*), people have learned to interpret television genres as primarily one or the other. Expository visual forms, such as documentary and news, are believed to reflect an external reality, or truth, unproblematically. Many advertisements, aiming to persuade primarily by extolling the virtues of a product, emulate this form.

As an expository form, *A New Beginning* worked to signify a particular version of reality. Its wholesome, upbeat, and optimistic message could be perceived as an accurate representation of Ronald Reagan and America. This was accomplished, in part, by framing the film as a documentary, as described in Chapter 2. The film also shared some characteristics with narrative. Individual images and some scenes were narratives that told a story, but the segments that composed *A New Beginning* were not arranged in a linear, sequential order. The overall structure of the exposition was poetic. Meaning was conveyed through metaphors, associations, and juxtapositions. This is not unusual for experimental or "art" films; it is more uncommon for political discourse.

The organization of *A New Beginning* corresponded to a shift of emphasis from narrative or exposition to poetic organization of political advertisements. The film's structure complemented the soft-sell approach to advertising used by the Reagan campaign managers throughout the 1984 campaign. They rejected the idea of hard-sell commercials, consisting principally of argumentative exposition or "talking heads" of candidates stating their positions for or against issues. Instead, they used state-of-the-art video techniques that only fleetingly addressed specific issues, but associated the candidate with positive images that resonated with the audience's needs and desires as identified by market research. Instead of using formal argument, they used predominantly mythic appeals that evoked emotion, facilitated identification, and associated Ronald Reagan with patriotic feelings about America. If the campaign film was the advertisement, Ronald Reagan was, indeed, the "product" being sold to a nation of consumers. He was reported to have quipped upon meeting the Tuesday Team, the illustrious group of advertising experts who were to run his campaign, "I heard that you were selling soap, and I thought that you might like to see the bar." (The comment is itself an advertising cliché.)[7]

The resultant emphasis was on formulas, clichés, and emotional advertising to sell Ronald Reagan to a public avid for consumption. This is not to say that no "formal" logic or argumentation occurs within *A New Beginning*. On the contrary, Ronald Reagan as narrator often performs this function. As an expository form, the film argues that it represents a social reality. It does so, however, primarily by creating a favorable psychological image, by fostering a positive impression or attitude. Persuasion through use of "irrefutable" logic, evidence, or "facts" is clearly subordinate.

Scene 1 of *A New Beginning* provides an excellent example of the way that the poetic organization of the film conveys meaning without requiring reflection and analysis. It begins conventionally with the date of Reagan's inauguration in 1980 on a black screen while he begins his oath of office. While the inauguration itself is obviously linear and sequential, the images that are interspersed are atemporal and have no overtly logical relationship to the words being spoken. The internal structure of this opening scene indicates the way that meaning is conveyed in *A New Beginning* through metaphor, association, and juxtaposition rather than through formal argument. The scene aims to create a mood, tone, or feeling that, as part of the image mosaic that composes the film, will contribute to the overall impression, or image, the viewer takes away from it. The meaning of visual advertisements is established by the viewer correlating image and product. Visual images connote certain qualities, or values that, by the participation of the viewer who is already familiar with their connotations, become transferred to the "product," that is, Ronald Reagan.[8]

In Scene 1, Ronald Reagan's figure precedes the other images which his voice explicates. His image, a re-presentation of past actuality, surrounds ordinary America and Americans; his voice conjures these images and ultimately, he explains their significance, "Yes, it was quite a day . . . a new beginning." This refers to both the inauguration and the images of Americans beginning a new day cross-cut within it. The qualities and values these images of a new day connote are transferred to Ronald Reagan. The initial image of a plow furrowing the earth in the early morning sun suggests growth, fertility, fecundity. It is a simple image, yet one evocative of America's agrarian roots; this is especially the case when the image is joined to that of a farmhouse. This too evokes a simple America untarnished by industry and technology. The cock crows, the flowers bloom, and there is work to be done, indicated by the dumptruck with an empty bed moving out of frame. A cowboy and his horse dissolve into a city laborer at work. Both country and city are unified, both are peopled by men at work. The laborer's upward pointing gesture is, like the previous sunlit images, an indication of optimism. Through the juxtaposition of these images and their connotations (and their unification through the implication of a beginning, a new day), Reagan is imbued with the positive qualities of traditional America: its fecundity, beauty, optimism, hope.

In addition to work, protection and defense, important themes throughout *A New Beginning*, are also suggested early in the scene. A traffic policemen, prominently wearing his badge, guides a group of construction workers across the street. This invites associations with law and order, particularly because the word "defend," spoken by the Chief Justice as Reagan takes his oath of office, accompanies this image. Then, Reagan's voice promises to "preserve and protect" and a wooded camp area appears on screen, where a group of children watch as a flag is being hoisted. This could create associations with Reagan as an environmentalist, implicitly mitigating criticism of him in this area. The flag is going up, as had the sun in the preceding images. It connotes freedom and patriotism, and in conjunction with the sun, productivity, hope, and a new day.

A close-up of one child's face is coupled with the word *defend*, suggesting the need to defend the nation's children, rather than "the Constitution of the United States," which is the continuation of this dialogue in the next shot. These words are paried with an image of the White House, the unifying center of political stability and authority. It links the images that have come before with Ronald Reagan and his presidency. The depiction of the White House dissolves into another image that positions Ronald Reagan securely within its confines, seated at his desk in the Oval Office.

Thus, this initial two-and-one-half-minute scene, composed of simple, even commonplace images, constructs a highly complex "image" of Ronald Reagan and what he represents: tradition, hope, productivity, defense, patriotism, innocence, the future, authority. These connections are not made verbally or through logical argument, but rather through the oral logic of poetic visual communication. Nor could these messages have been so powerfully conveyed in two and one-half minutes of a speech.

Overall, the film aimed to create an impression of spiritual rebirth, of optimism, patriotism, and productivity across the land. Most important, this renewal was inextricably related to Ronald Reagan by juxtaposing images with conventional, generally positive associations and the voice/image of Ronald Reagan.

Like the initial scene, none of the images that composed the various segments of the film created this impression through formal argument. None of the scenes following the inauguration were arranged in chronological or sequential order to build a persuasive argument. The attempt upon Reagan's life, for instance, which occurred in March of 1981, was presented well after later events such as his trip to Korea. Scene 5, entirely structured to follow Lee Greenwood's song, "God Bless the USA," made little attempt to establish internal temporal or linear logical relations, and itself had no temporal relation to the rest of the film. Together the scenes, differentiated by their themes, made up the fragments of the image mosaic.

A New Beginning as Visual Cliché

Although *A New Beginning* was structured as a poetic-image mosaic, this formal departure from traditional political discourse was accompanied by familiar and instantly recognizable images. Reagan communicated to the public with familiar, reassuring images: not simply depictions, but visual clichés and stereotypes whose implications and associations have become commonplace, given, beyond question. The clichéd images that constructed much of the film already had an emotional (if vague) meaning associated with them. They invoked conventional associations; they were tied to a meaning that did not require reflection and analysis in order to be discerned.

A case in point is the usage of dark and light. Michael Osborn writes that light and dark are archetypal metaphors with persuasive power because of their "double associations:" light and dark are associated with prominent features of experience, which are themselves symbolic expressions of basic human motivations.[9] For example, light is positively valued because it can be associated with all of the concepts that people associate with the spatial metaphor "up": happiness, consciousness, control, goodness, rationality, high status (which themselves symbolize the basic human motives of survival and development).[10] In filmic symbolism, light implies knowledge, goodness, life, hope, and beginning. It is one of the primary symbols of the Western tradition, as in the Bible where God said, "Let there be light."

Such imagery is pervasive throughout Western art and literature, so much so that it has become cliché. Accordingly, light is a central motif in *A New Beginning*, one that is also compatible with the many religious associations in the film. It begins in darkness; the first image is light, as the brilliant sun blazes in the sky. Throughout, the images in the film are bathed in the sun's rays. Reagan's America is bright and sunny, that is, good, happy, healthy, optimistic. For the most part, the film is packed with familiar, positive clichés: babies, smiling children, flowers, a wedding, people hugging, touching, smiling, looking up, gesturing up, building, working. All of these images have appeared time and again on greeting cards, on television, in movies. They invoke knee-jerk associations with the way people "remember" it to be, or, more likely, with the way that they would like it to have been.

Both the aesthetic use of light and dark and the content of the images that construct the film are clichés. The American family that appears in scenes 5 and 8, for instance, is a cliché. In scene 5, the family is onscreen as singer Lee Greenwood pays homage to America; "I thank my lucky stars to be living here today." There are two parents and two children, predictably a boy and a girl. The girl clutches a teddy bear while the boy helps his father carry a rug out of the house; the boy manages to hold a baseball glove in his hand at the same time. The house is surrounded by a white picket fence; the yard has rosebushes. Later in the film, as Reagan discusses improvements in the economy in scene 8, this same family reappears, although they are wearing different clothes. This time, the wife steps out of a house with red brick stairs and a walkway. She tousles her son's hair and smiles at her husband, who this time is singlehandedly carrying a rug into a house that boasts a "Sold" sign in front of it. There is a fence around this new home too, but this second house is bigger than the first one. As Reagan asserts that there has been an increase in the consumer's ability to purchase cars, the husband walks toward a shiny red truck parked in the now spacious yard. A man wearing a suit and tie greets him as the daughter, still clutching her doll from the first scene, jumps into the truck. Both men shake hands, pat each other on the back, and walk amiably toward the truck. Either a business deal has been struck, or an advertisement for insurance has been smuggled into the film.

This is the traditional family from 1950s television shows which, even then, bore little resemblance to the actual state of affairs. It is an idyllic vision, but a familiar model to many middle-class Americans. There are two parents, one child of each sex, and traditional roles. The young boy carries a baseball mitt while his sister has a doll. The wife does no physical labor, but she offers encouragement while her husband carries a carpet into the house. The white picket fence, the shrubbery in the yard, the new, bigger house, and the new truck are familiar images of the American Dream; the image is easy to consume. Everything is harmonious here. There is no tension apparent and the viewer need not think much about it in order to understand it. It brings feeling rather than thought to the fore; it predisposes the viewer to a favorable attitude. The sun shines, the family is smiling, they are prosperous, they are upwardly mobile: all in the context of Ronald Reagan's improvements, of which he reminds the viewer as this scene plays. Through association, this cliché favorably orients the viewer to Ronald Reagan; it is functional precisely because it lacks substantive, heuristic meaning other than that provided by its positioning within the film.

What is most important is that this cliché, and all of the simple, mythic images that permeate *A New Beginning*, have no meaning in and of themselves. Even the film's title is a verbal cliché. No information, particularly no insight, is provided. There is merely a repetition of traditional cultural images that echo and reproduce the status quo. These images are, however, reassuring. They are pleasurable because they are so effortlessly recognizable. They reinforce conventional images of social reality and one's middle-class place in it. These clichés serve as points of orientation; their connotations, implications, and associations appear to be self-evident and need not be questioned. They are effective, moreover, because they illustrate the more pragmatic, "actual" claims made throughout the film. Claims that the economy is better, for instance, made by Ronald Reagan and persons interviewed throughout the film, are supported with these visual clichés.

Stereotypes

Through use of visual cliché, Reagan invoked symbolic common-places with which he associated himself; further, through use of another type of visual cliché, the stereotype, A New Beginning provided figures with which the viewer could identify. These figures represented a cross-section of Americans whose support Reagan wanted in the coming election. It was important, in order to gain a consensus and to unify the political "center," to provide stereotypical images of "we" Americans that could serve as points of identification for the home viewing audience. Through identification, people place themselves within groups or movements; identification makes social life possible.[11]

Stereotypes represented a recognizable world with familiar situations and social positions. Through identification with these representatives of social groups, the viewer shared in their experiences. The persons interviewed in the film were echoes of ordinary "people on the street" who appear in advertisements or on the evening news. These people are conventionally assumed to have no vested interest in the subject under discussion, and supposedly they represent the climate of opinion surrounding an issue.[12] Their opinions and interests, which reflected favorably upon the Reagan administration, could be accepted as relevant definitions of the social and historical situation.

The people interviewed in A New Beginning asserted that America was experiencing an economic and spiritual recovery, and implied or directly attributed this state of affairs to Ronald Reagan. In this way, they functioned rhetorically as demonstrative proofs that supported, or authenticated, the otherwise unverifiable claims made throughout the film.[13] At the same time, because they were merely people on the street expressing their opinions, their words did not have to be verifiable.

The social and occupational groups that appeared onscreen suggested that Reagan aimed to reach the middle and working classes. Lower- and upper-class stereotypes were conspicuous by their absence. Interviews were conducted with professional persons, women, blacks, a Hispanic, and the elderly; images of farmers, factory workers, and construction workers also permeated the film. These constituencies were important targets for the Republican party. Laborers, in particular, have traditionally been aligned with the Democratic party, and Reagan's attempt to woo the blue-collar workers was obvious in *A New Beginning*.

Laborers predominate in scene 4, which is the first sequence of interviews with "the people," all of which coalesce around the theme that there is a new feeling of pride and patriotism in America. There are three blue-collar workers, one black man in a business suit, a young woman with a faintly Hispanic accent, and one noticeably nondescript middle-aged white male representative. The workers are located by clothing and background. The first is in a factory or warehouse; he wears a solid blue uniform, and people are busily engaged in work in the background. He asserts, "The bottom line with President Reagan is that he has brought back respect to the White House." Similarly, a young black worker, dressed in a T-shirt and located at a building construction site, announces, "I feel more patriotic towards my country and I feel more proud to be an American. A third worker, also located at a noisy construction site and wearing a hard hat, forcefully declares in a strong colloquial accent, "He put me to work, he's gonna keep me there. The man did a good job, and I hope he's gonna go another four years. God Bless America."

The man insists that "Ronald Reagan" put him to work, while he blesses "America." Patriotism is explicitly related here to economic advantage, while both are linked to support for Ronald Reagan, who is rendered indistinguishable from the country he represents. All of the people interviewed here celebrate the general attitude in the country, the "new" spirit of pride proclaimed by George Bush. As stereotypes, they imply that both blue-collar workers and minorities share a positive attitude towards America and, by implication, Ronald Reagan. Both verbal statements and visual cues, too, suggest that this attitude is warranted because of economic gains. The laborers are not only employed, but they are interviewed at bustling workplaces. Their activity suggests growth, production, and development; the predominance of images of workers building, making, and doing throughout the film serves as a metaphor for America's "new" beginning, and as a concrete effort to obtain the allegiance of this bloc of voting Americans.

All in all, this scene appears to be directed to working-class Americans, with an unspoken promise of upward mobility. The voices of a foreign woman and a black man sporting a suit and tie echo the sentiments of the laborers. Their expressed satisfaction and pride suggest that minorities, like blue-collar workers, can prosper in Ronald Reagan's America. Their interests are, moreover, made to coincide with those of the "average" American, as this scene concludes with the remarks of a stereotypical "everyman" who cannot easily be located in terms of occupation, social, or ethnic group. Even the green-grass background suggests neutrality. He represents the political middle, and his presence provides assurance that Reagan supporters are mainstream Americans whose ranks include the members of specific interest groups. His remark, "I even hear songs on the radio, TV now" serves as a transition to scene 5, which consists of a patriotic song accompanied by images about America.

The next group of interviewees appears in scene 7. These men and women are middle-class representatives whose concerns mirror those of the majority of Americans. Their comments vaguely address issues such as defense and the economy; for the most part, they offer testimonials to the theme that the economy is better. They laud the economic improvements made by the Reagan administration, which, they assert, have made their lives better. Consumerism is the focus here; they are pleased because they are able to buy more with Ronald Reagan as president. One woman mentions that "people are traveling more, business is better, people going on vacations, and they are spending more money." These people celebrate the transformation in social status indicated by leisure-time activities and monetary gain. The possibility of upward mobility convinces them that the economy must be better; one man even mentions the "facts" that unemployment and interest rates are down. He neglected to add, however, that they remained higher than they had been when Reagan first took office.

This scene appeals to those who identify with the more affluent middle classes. While scene 4 implies that people are gainfully employed because Ronald Reagan is in office, those who appear in scene 7 seem to be more preoccupied with advancement. A golfer (another indication of the leisure time available to prosperous Americans) notes that "the people" are getting back to work. Both he, and the others who appear in this scene, are thus separated from the legions of the unemployed. They praise Ronald Reagan because they are able to have and to do more.

The representation of black Americans also merits consideration. They appear in the army, but none are present in the rural and suburban scenes of traditional America. Two out of the three black men who are interviewed are wearing suits, although two appear in the first "blue-collar" scene, and only one in the predominantly middle-class scene 7. It is apparent that Reagan wanted to appeal to black Americans, but primarily upwardly mobile ones who were likely to vote. (Even so, Mondale won the majority of the black vote in 1984.) In scene 7, a black man wearing a suit, who is positioned against an urban background, says, "We're gonna be better off in the long run." It was left unclear whether he was referring to black Americans, all Americans, or both.

No black women at all appeared in the film, although Reagan's weakest constituencies were women and blacks. It was also suggestive of the Reagan administration's less-than-liberated attitude toward women that only one could be identified by occupational group, and none in terms of social class. One businesswoman was photographed against an urban-street background, wearing a foulard tie, which is stereotypical attire for businesswomen (scene 9). Her remark deserves special attention:

> He's been on television, what have I heard, twenty-six times? Talking to us about what he's doing? Now that's . . . he's not doing that for any other reason than to make it real clear. And if anybody has any question about where he's headed, it's their fault. Maybe they don't have a television.

This woman turned one of Reagan's weaknesses into a perceived strength, for he had given fewer press conferences in his first term than any other president in the age of television. She also blamed those who were unaware of Reagan's position on the issues for not having a television—an unintended comment on Reagan's primarily televisual presidency and on the dominance of television in contemporary culture. Her words gained added emphasis because the screen faded to black after she spoke.

All other women were photographed against a blurred or floral background and were dressed anonymously. One woman (scene 4) was even standing in front of a stream of rippling water. These settings were certainly picturesque, but they contrasted markedly with the building sites, golf courses, and noisy city streets that located the men in the world of work.

The elderly also received their own special section of the film, tied to Ronald Reagan's commitment to Social Security. An elderly man commended Reagan for getting inflation down (throughout the film, Reagan is commended personally for events over which he had little control), and a woman asserted that he was a "caring man." Again, these were stereotypical notions of male and female (and elderly) concerns. These easily recognizable and identifiable figures presented what was, for Republican purposes, a well-rounded picture of America. Like visual clichés, they provided points of orientation for many voting Americans who identified with these groups. Most importantly, not much reflection was required. These people espoused values that were representative of social groups and their interests. Middle-class women, black men, workers, and the elderly appeared disproportionately in comparison to other sections of the population.

The poetic organization of *A New Beginning* used metaphor, juxtaposition, and association to render its visual clichés and stereotypes meaningful. The people who appeared onscreen functioned to create the illusion of consensus; they represented the Republicans' image of the political center, which they wanted to gather into their fold. Just like visual clichés, these simplistic stereotypes served to mask conflict and diversity of opinion and interests. The film prereflectively and preanalytically conveyed the message that America was experiencing a patriotic awakening and an economic resurgence, and that Ronald Reagan was personally responsible for these events. This was the self-image of America, and Americans, constructed by Ronald Reagan and *A New Beginning*.

7 Critically Reframing
A New Beginning

You may hold that there is no essential difference between sensory image and mythic image. And both may be treated merely as rhetorical reinforcements of ideas. Hence, all three would be "ideological," in the sense that, where they gain social currency in formal expression, they can be shown to represent the particular perspective of some more or less limited group, to sanction special interests in terms of universal validity.
—Kenneth Burke, Rhetoric of Motives

A New Beginning exemplified the Republicans' ability to take advantage of the differences between the reception of visual and verbal communication forms in contemporary American culture. Television, among other visual communication forms, has marked a break from previous ways of knowing and experiencing the world. The dominance of television as cultural center marks a transition from a modern to a postmodern society. Modernization, associated with the Industrial Revolution and the rise of entrepreneurial capitalism, was characterized by processes such as industrialization, urbanization, the growth of bureaucracy, and a print-oriented culture. Postmodernism is a term that describes the effects of the transformation from entrepreneurial to monopoly capitalism and the end of the Industrial Revolution; postmodern American culture is marked by deindustrialization, a shift from production to consumption, a continuing proliferation of technology, and the entrenchment of visual communication, resulting in the prevailing culture of the image.[1]

The technologies of film and television have heralded an historically new mass experience, where there has been a shift from a literate to a postliterate culture, from a newspaper- to a television-centered system of communication, from language-based to iconic symbolism.[2] A postmodern visual culture has supplanted a print culture, with different epistemological consequences. Print is a conceptual medium that can convey nuanced arguments and complexities; it can thus facilitate reflection, analysis, discussion and debate. Visual media are essentially formulaic, dramatic efforts to intensify the immediacy of emotion and experience.[3] Print requires discursive skills to be comprehended, while visual media are visceral. Print media are believed to refer to reality, while visual media are believed to reflect and even create it.

A New Beginning was significant as a masterly project that brought specifically televisual communication strategies to presidential political filmmaking. It remains a landmark event in televisual political communication. In the guise of entertaining television, the film defined both Ronald Reagan and the broad themes that shaped his campaign. It marked the first time that a visual presentation was substituted for the nominating speech at a national political convention, and it established a central place for the political campaign film as the vehicle that precedes the candidate's acceptance speech at the convention. In 1984, the networks' decisions whether or not to air A New Beginning were controversial; by 1988, both Republican and Democratic candidates were introduced to the public by way of their campaign films.

While political speeches are often mediated to the public through television, and while political speeches also make use of myths and clichés, I have contended throughout this study that A New Beginning is a qualitatively different mode of address than is a political speech. The film was a specifically televisual presentation, one which used the conventions, perceived capacities, and audience expectations of the medium to fullest advantage. Reagan and his media advisers were acutely aware of how the requirements of televisual communication differed from those of oratory. An orator may require fifteen minutes to argue a point; in fifteen minutes of film, the candidate's ethos, message, and theme can be established through the strategic interplay of words, music, and pictures. In the political campaign film, words can be supported with visual "proofs," just as visual images can overpower and render words unnecessary. Moreover, musical backdrops establish an emotional tone that directs feelings about the words and images on screen. Not only are more multimodal channels of communication open in a film than a speech, but sound and pictures can communicate by association, implication, and innuendo. It is difficult to lie with pictures, which do not assert so much as suggest, and whose meaning remains on some level ambiguous. In the political campaign film, then, there is more freedom to mislead than there is in a political campaign speech.

The role of Ronald Reagan, the "Great Communicator," as mediator of the Republican message cannot be underestimated. As an ex-actor and professional narrator, Reagan knew how to exploit the medium. More so than any other presidential candidate before him, Reagan was able to master the relaxed and nuanced conversational style so effective on television. Unlike a platform speaker, Reagan the television orator aimed to reach people in the privacy of their living rooms. A subtle lifting of the eyebrow, a nod of the head, a wink or a smile were artful rhetorical devices. Even when reading from a teletape, Reagan appeared to be engaged in a sincere and spontaneous talk with the viewer.

A New Beginning did, indeed, play to public perceptions of Reagan's strengths as a president and a charismatic persona. He spoke to Americans from the Oval Office; he presided over political ceremonies; he allowed viewers a glimpse of how he spent his leisure time on his ranch. Footage of the assassination attempt reminded viewers of the event that had made him a figure of mythic stature. Camera angles, lighting, and the juxtaposition of shots all worked together to make him appear to be a heroic, larger-than-life figure, yet these devices may not have been so suasory had they been used with another candidate. Reagan's ability to project qualities that were both "presidential" and ordinary; his peculiar combination of movie-star qualities with those of the cowboy; and his ability to be perceived to be a leader and a man of the people: all were part of his political appeal.

Most important, Reagan appeared to mediate conflicts and contradictions in the American psyche. He mediated polarities such as moralism and materialism, liberalism and conservatism, the individual and the community. He was able to create the illusion of American omnipotence and prosperity, and to create the impression of presidential strength and leadership that coincided with a resurgent populism. Reagan, the consummate political performer, was able to play to the voters' preferences. His image became inextricably associated with America's renewed patriotic attitude. Reagan as symbol was able to restore the illusion of unity and consensus, thus providing momentum for this attitude.

Ronald Reagan, as conveyed through television, established a rapport with the American people that transcended his particular policies. As evidenced by the oft-repeated observation, many people liked him while disagreeing with his political positions, thus earning him the title of the "Teflon President." Even more ironically, his personal history did not coincide with his political persona. Though he spoke for family and religious values, he was divorced, had never seen one of his grandchildren, was estranged from his two youngest children, and did not attend church.

In addition to providing insight into Reagan's political persona, the style and structure of the campaign film illustrate the art of presidential communication in a media age. Television images can impress themselves on the viewer prior to logical processes of reflection and analysis; thus, the film's poetic mosaic structure provided a form within which reassuring, easily recognizable clichés and stereotypes became associated with Ronald Reagan and American resurgence. Moreover, the film's occlusion of the frames which differentiated genres, levels, and spaces of televisual discourse allowed the Republicans to constitute the reality they were ostensibly allowing to appear. In particular, the admixture of documentary and fictional film forms and styles, as well as the confusion of boundaries between the film and the live convention of which it was a part, provided impetus for the viewer to interpret it in terms of "reality" that existed outside of the film. The intersection of story and discourse, and the creation of pseudodiscourse where Ronald Reagan appeared to address the viewer directly, indicated a reality not bounded by the television frame.

The Republicans exploited the unifying and centralizing capacity of television by rendering different ways of knowing and comprehending television discourse indistinguishable. It became difficult to discriminate immediate and mediated experience, reality and fantasy, history and myth. Although Reagan's policies benefited the few rather than the many, through media manipulations the Republicans managed to create the illusion of unity and consensus. A New Beginning constructed a community of ordinary Americans, mediated by Ronald Reagan who was both character (one of the people), and narrator (their authoritative leader). The film proposed the rebirth of this community; its larger claim, that America had experienced a "new beginning," was supported by a fiction of the real and a fiction of discourse about this real.

The Republicans were persuasive, furthermore, as a consequence of their televised re-presentation of familiar myths. Myths enable reality to be typified, reflected upon, and constituted as coherent and noncontradictory. The film provided a mythic framework of rebirth, a familiar story throughout Western art, literature, and history. Its vision of America, and Ronald Reagan as humble yet heroic savior, resonated with similar narratives in American mythology and history. The Republicans also used the myth of rebirth to propose the rebirth of American myths, myths that concerned the nature and purpose of America, the conflict between the individual and the community, and the role of the president. This redefinition enabled them to construct a new identity for "the people," as opposing versions of American myths were revitalized to accord with the demands of modernity wile reaffirming tradition.

Television was a particularly apt medium for such a task. Television is a primary perpetrator of myths, and its myths are believed to be representations of reality, more so than those of other forms of discourse. Television's mode of presentation is marked by a predominance of discursive space, defined by its qualities of perceived liveness, immediacy, and a direct mode of address from narrator to viewer. Televised myths are re-presented to the audience, and an attempt is made to convince the audience that these are appropriate to their context (In the case of the film, the actual, historical "frame" which these myths articulate).

In *A New Beginning*, myths and clichés articulated "reality." The visual portrait of America and Americans was filled out by anecdotal "evidence": interviews, short narratives, photographic testimony, newspaper headlines. These televisual demonstrations, on the surface, appeared to be cogent replications of a plausible reality. They offered reassuring interpretations of what people already "knew" to be the case, and in this way, unified viewers around this central position of knowledge. What people "knew" to have been the case in the past was re-presented in the present, in order to direct them toward the future.

Unlike ceremonial political campaign discourse, which is primarily argumentative though perhaps based upon myths, *A New Beginning* was primarily mythic although it had an argumentative dimension. The film undermined the rhetorically argumentative, and elevated the mythic dimensions of political discourse. Because its rhetorical, logically argumentative dimension was framed by myth, there were no obvious grounds for dissension and debate. Myth superseded rhetoric, so that premises remained implicit and unquestioned.

A New Beginning, unlike traditional campaign oratory, did not appear to be an argument about ends or the best means to attain them. Because the ends were already agreed upon, the viewer who rejected the film was left without a positive alternative. Its mythic rhetoric did not allow dissension from within. Myths can only be appraised from a position outside, but the nature of myth is to deny that such a position exists.

A New Beginning, particularly as it was interplayed with other political discourses of the Reagan Administration and other cultural discourses, effectively masked the indeterminacy and relativization of meaning, and accordingly, the role of the audience in the production of this meaning. Myths and clichés anchored the social order because they were unquestioningly recognized and accepted. The positions of the viewers were thus secure: they were spoken to, they were addressed, and they could recognize themselves through this call. The viewers who consumed these images were able to participate in "social communion," yet it was a communion that denied difference, distance, alternative frames in the representation of a unified and all encompassing "we."[4] This "we," spoken by both Ronald Reagan and the ordinary Americans in the film, defined an American community that did not exist other than through its representation, its simulation. This unified group embodied a set of beliefs, values, attitudes and interests that coincided with those of the Reagan administration. The film's mode of presentation was thus able to mask class differences, contradictory realities, and the social positions of the viewers as consumers who were exploited by producers (including the invisible "producers" of Ronald Reagan and *A New Beginning*: the affluent who supported his election bid with their campaign contributions, and who benefited from his policies).

A New Beginning offered its viewers security. Its interpretive frame posited a reality that was familiar, intelligible, and reassuring, so long as the viewer subjected herself to the authority of Ronald Reagan. That he offered a pseudodiscourse, that the film allowed no space for interaction, that Ronald Reagan was presented as pure image, did not seem to matter to the majority of voting Americans. They responded to and identified with the image of the audience that Ronald Reagan reflected.

However, the viewer who accepted this simulacrum, who recognized his own image in the images portrayed, became disempowered rather than empowered. The viewer became framed by, but could not frame, the television images. The viewer lost discursive control in the production of her position vis-à-vis the film. Political reality was no longer created and negotiated through discourse, but its control became the province of the few, those with the position, authority, and technical skills. In this sense, Ronald Reagan offered Americans an image that was simultaneously a mirror and a screen.

In effect, the contemporary political campaign film, as a genre that supersedes oratory, suggests that political discourse subverts rather than extends democratic processes based upon equal participation and informed and reasoned dialogue. It promulgates an ideology not by informing, but by entertaining, by providing mythic images that evoke common beliefs and values, and by manipulating the interpretive frames by which meaning and sense is accrued. It uses a means of communication that is only partly linguistic. Its techniques reproduce and mimic the language of "the people," but the people do not themselves use these techniques to respond. Televisual communication is available only to those in control of resources, capital, specialized knowledge, and skills. As a result, there is no common ground of discourse on which the electorate can discuss and debate. Information is placed in the hands of the few who dispose of it as they will. In the case of Ronald Reagan, his use of modern communication techniques masked the contradictions that permeated the social, economic, and cultural milieu: those between the capitalist ethic and alternative realities, between tradition and modernity, between producers and consumers in society. He offered *A New Beginning* as another object for consumption. It promised happiness and fulfillment in exchange for complicity in the acceptance of prefabricated meaning.

Reagan and his strategists presented a danger to the democratic principles they purported to maintain. They made capitalism more rather than less exploitative, by constructing an illusory unity while perpetuating class divisions. The contradiction between the mythic ideal and the real world of experience remained; it could not be wished away by a film or a campaign. The film offered a self-confirming myth through which the individual and the collective could locate themselves within ongoing events. However, it left no place for those to whom the myth did not speak, those for whom this myth did not provide a satisfying and plausible explanation of their experience. It worked well for the upper class, the elite who would rather remain invisible in a society that espoused a myth of equality, but it did not work so well for those on the bottom of the socioeconomic scale who did not prosper with the "rebirth" of the myths that guided and defined American society.

An argument in popular culture studies that stresses the poly-semic nature of meaning claims that meaning can never be deter-mined from above. Although dominant ideology tries to reproduce itself, culture is always a site of struggle for meaning. Hegemony must be fought for and won. Thus, as first explicated by Stuart Hall, every text has three possible readings: a "preferred" reading (which expresses dominant ideology); a negotiated reading (where viewers accept dominant meanings, but adapt them to their own interests); and an oppositional reading (where readers subvert the meanings of the dominant ideology).[5]

My argument that readers can be "inside" or "outside" myths supports Hall's view. However, my analysis of *A New Beginning* indi-cates the increasing difficulty of reading from "outside" the domi-nant ideology when psychological, political, cultural, and technolog-ical apparatus work to keep the reader/viewer inside. The postmodern culture of the image, which has supplanted the culture of the word, marks a paradigmatic shift from a rational to narrative worldview across American culture. Walter Fisher distinguishes between the two: the materials of the rational paradigm are "self-evi-dent propositions, demonstrations and proofs, the verbal expressions of certain and probably knowing." The materials of the narrative paradigm are "symbols, signs of consubstantiation, and good rea-sons."[6] In the first case, standards for evaluating political discourse are the principles of formal logic and argumentation. In the latter, standards for evaluation are narrative probability and fidelity: consis-tency with morality and commonsense understandings, and corre-spondence to "reality."

One way to do an oppositional reading of a film such as *A New Beginning*, then, is to shift paradigms; it is to read a visual text that is structured according to the principles of the narrative paradigm from a critical-rational standpoint, which applies standards of formal rea-soning and argumentation. Yet, such a standpoint may be merely irrelevant, a verbal anachronism is a visual culture. Another way is to deconstruct the "story" by pointing to its arbitrary rhetorical nature. Only by making the "invisible" rhetorical nature of political films apparent will they be read, responded to, and evaluated as argu-ments.

However, to do oppositional readings of mass-mediated texts would entail a major reframing of many Americans' experience of themselves, the media, and the political world around them. Cultural momentum militates against such a shift. The political manipulation of the media continues, and there is little indication that viewers have become correspondingly more savvy. In 1988, George Bush emulated the Reagan strategy (and even replayed many of the same images) and was elected president, while loser Michael Dukakis was widely chastised for not heeding the advice of his media "handlers." At best, there is hope that the divergent but equally suasory uses to which candidates put television will give voters pause to reevaluate their relationships to televisual political discourse.

8 Methodological Implications

Throughout this study, I have attempted to provide insight into the ways that the Republicans made use of the political campaign film in order to serve their ideological ends in a culture increasingly oriented toward visual communication forms.

Analysis of televisual political communication is particularly important given television's pervasiveness in modern mass-mediated campaigns. This project contributes to the growing corpus of work that aims to understand the complex interrelations of televisual production and reception within a particular sociocultural context. Such a task is complicated by the fact that televisual-political-cultural texts do not fit into discrete disciplinary boundaries. To describe *A New Beginning*, I made use of insights from contemporary cultural, political, television, film, and rhetorical criticisms. The main ideal of criticism, according to Kenneth Burke, is to use all there is to use.[1] Not being bounded by a disciplinary frame enabled my own analysis to become all the richer, and the result showed how these critical areas can contribute to one another.

Though this study is firmly rooted in the rhetorical tradition, and builds upon rhetorical methods of analysis, it is a product of cross-fertilization of ideas from many different traditions. Much of the theoretical work is drawn from communication theory, cultural studies, Marxist and ideological analysis, the study of myth and narrative, semiotics and poststructuralism, all of which coalesce in a mode of analysis known as postmodernism. Postmodernism is simultaneously defined as a phase of late capitalism and as a particular cultural context marked by the breakdown and blurring of categories, whether in art, culture, or academic enterprises.[2] Thus my method borrows with impunity from fields outside of rhetoric, just as my analysis of *A New Beginning* locates it as a postmodern film. As such, it (1) blurs boundaries between different televisual genres, (2) juxtaposes contradictory myths and images mediated by Ronald Reagan, and (3) elevates the simulacrum, the image made for television which refers to nothing beyond itself. Yet, my project remains principally *rhetorical* criticism; its main concern is with how *A New Beginning*'s meanings were made, how they were presented, and how they invited particular interpretations from an audience. It makes use of the symbolic forms that characterize filmic and television discourse, but with an eye to their persuasive import. In this way it moves beyond a semiotic analysis that, because of its basis in structural linguistics, has proved problematic when analyzing non-verbal images, to an emphasis on rhetoric as a more appropriate model to analyze televisual communication.

Indeed, much contemporary criticism is itself postmodern in that it is marked by an overlap of previously discrete realms of inquiry. All such critical approaches share the same concern: to understand the relationship between cultural texts, their social and/or political contexts, and the processes whereby audiences make sense out of them. Rhetoric, understood as all symbolic behavior designed to communicate, is applicable as an organizing principle for these critical realms of inquiry. Scholars in both scientific and human-istic fields have increasingly become aware of the rhetorical dimen-sions in their objects of analysis. To communicate is to use symbols; which symbols are used, when, and how has an influence on how meaning is interpreted. The meaning of any symbol, or representa-tion, is conditioned by one's language and culture; thus it is rhetori-cal.

The study assumes, then, that meanings are socially constructed and that mass media, as primary promoters and circulators of mean-ings, contribute to the construction of social reality for its partici-pants. Yet, though we experience the world through symbols that condition our knowledge, these symbols do not have one univocal meaning. Rather, meanings in mass-mediated texts are multidimen-sional. Readers bring many experiences to bear on them, though the producers of cultural texts may attempt to delimit and control the variety of possible interpretations.

At the least, rhetorical forms influence definitions of social real-ity; at most, they shape the social order that becomes "reality." Either way, it is the critic's responsibility to move beyond description of the processes by which meanings are created through televisual commu-nication, and to evaluate these processes in order to generate dis-course about discourse. The critic's task is not to just explicate, but to assess public discourse, to hold a speaker responsible for the words she speaks or the images she promotes which portray a version of reality. This task has been complicated in the modern media age, where a text may not have a single "speaker," where it may be difficult to locate the boundaries of a single text, or where arguments may be implied by images rather than verbally asserted. Such a state makes the rhetorical criticism of televisual political communication all the more important. Democracy is premised upon reasoned discourse by which people decide the best course of action; yet it is possible for genres such as the contemporary televisual political campaign film to silence discourse. Such texts use arguments that circumvent reason as they channel an otherwise heterogeneous multiplicity of cultural discourses into a single reassuring and coherent image.

Rhetorical analyses, concerned with the relationship of a discourse to its audience, typically focus on one of the following points of entry: the situation or context in which a message is constructed, the speaker or author of a message, or the text itself. In this analysis, which I term textual frame analysis, I examine the interrelationships of context, source, text, and audience. I consider *A New Beginning* as a cultural text where all of these categories overlap and interpenetrate one another. At the same time, textual frame analysis draws upon and extends some of its critical predecessors that emphasize one or the other entry point.

I consider the Reagan film as an exemplar of the contemporary televisual political campaign film; my textual frame analysis is a form of generic criticism that emphasizes the historical context of the film. Similarly, textual frame analysis has common points with mass-movement criticism, which focuses on the social milieu that gives rise to group action. Textual frame analysis likewise shares concerns with studies of situated texts; the latter emphasize context by focusing on the predominance of the image as a condition of late capitalism. My method draws from critical methods (such as Goffman's dramaturgy), which emphasize the source of a rhetorical message in order to determine the social reality that is created; and from metaphoric or structuralist methods, which are concerned with a close analysis of the language or visual images which structure the text itself.

Yet, all of the above approaches suffer from their emphasis upon one or the other points of entry; they do not attend sufficiently to the interrelation of source, message, channel, receiver and context and thus cannot dispel the gap between production and reception processes in the making of meaning. With textual frame analysis, the addition of another concept, framing, helps to explain how context, source, text, and audience interact in the production of the "meaning" of A New Beginning.

Thus, I examined a cultural artifact from different perspectives, or "frames." While one of the basic assumptions of this study is that it is impossible to know any text in its entirety, examining it from a number of different angles can shed more insight into its character than from one position alone. I combined critical perspectives that are not typically associated with one another but that were necessary to understand the contemporary televisual political campaign film. Overall, I examined the interrelations of the framing, context, content, and form in the production and reception of the film; in each chapter, I moved from theory to concrete analysis. My method was arrived at in the course of repeated viewing of the film, a process that enabled me to formulate, test, and sometimes discard ideas and approaches to the material.

More specifically, I began with a discussion of the way that the Republicans used framing to create a "reality," then I placed the film within its sociohistorical context to explore the ideology of this constructed frame. This analysis of the film's ideology helped explain the way that a cultural text produced a particular kind of knowledge for the viewer, one which was in the interests of the Reagan administration. This led me to ask the question, "How is this ideology communicated by a visual communication form?" I shifted my perspective to the text itself, and found that myths expressed ideology. Myth superseded discursive rhetoric as its primary mode of communication. Myth was particularly effective because the medium, television, is more suited to circulating cultural myths than to substantive argument. Myths, like television images, do not require reflection and analysis to be understood.

The film's mythic frame of rebirth communicated its ideological objectives. Because myths are themselves ideological, a closer examination of the particular myths that structured the film, in association with their occurrence at a particular historical juncture, helped explain the film's appeal to its audience. Finally, from an even closer vantage point I examined its visual clichés, the simple mythic images that provoked a positive emotional reflex, thus anchoring the reality framed by the film. A flag being raised, for instance, is a loaded symbol that evokes a multitude of mythic associations: patriotism, the glory of America, optimism, positive transformation. Television can convey such a message in a second; the viewer can make these associations without having to reason through them.

All of these tools helped explain why *A New Beginning* was a persuasive communication form; together, they underscored the extent to which the Republicans were able to make use of the visual media to serve their rhetorical ends.

Chapter 1, where I discuss framing, makes the greatest theoretical contribution to the analysis of the contemporary televisual political campaign film. This section also demonstrates the utility of combining rhetorical criticism and communication theory. I rely upon the work of communication theorists such as Gregory Bateson and Erving Goffman to examine the concept of framing in relation to *A New Beginning*. Both suggest that it is through "frames" that all experience is organized and rendered coherent; thus, the way that the film was framed contributed to the viewers' interpretations of it. Framing, in addition to historical context, form, and content, must be considered in order to understand the film.

In the case of the televisual political campaign film, framing is particularly important, given that the experience is mediated through a television or film frame. As Bateson notes, frames are metacommunicative; they implicitly define messages as real or imaginary, fact or fantasy, mediated or unmediated.[3] The relationship between frame and message may, however, be quite complex. Bateson cites play as an example of an event where a denotatively "real" message becomes bracketed, or reframed as fantasy. "Playful" behaviors are simulations of denotative messages; in other words, messages that are framed as "play" take on an as-if status. Television, like play, simulates a primary message. However, television is dis-play. Messages that are inherently fictional become reframed as real or true. The television medium is a self-contained world that works to establish the authority and authenticity of its messages, be they the "objective" referential reality of genres such as news and documentary, or the "subjective" symbolic reality of genres such as dramas and advertisements.

Visual events, then, are provided with meaning through the metacommunicative frame of television; within this frame different genres of televisual discourse are believed primarily to denote or connote a reality. *A New Beginning*, however, a political campaign film first presented on television as a substitute for a speech, is indicative of the Republicans' attempts to merge the frames that typically differentiate different genres, levels, and spaces of televisual discourse.

"Documentary" and "fictional" genres, "live" and prerecorded events, and even the spaces that separated the viewer from the event appeared to be indistinguishable.

Most important, the voice and figure of Ronald Reagan provided the unifying point of reference for all of the different forms and levels of representation. As narrator and character, both within and outside of the film, Reagan became imbued with a special authority to which all of the other voices and images became subordinated. This strategy enabled him to create a "fiction of discourse," a fiction that enabled him to appear to be addressing the audience from a position of knowledge.

The Republicans did their best to ensure that A New Beginning would be favorably received. It offered no controversy, it offended no one who was included in its representations, and it conveyed a slanted view of the Reagan presidency. If the film was a harbinger of the future of political discourse, this study has provided some analytic tools that reveal the moral dilemmas and ethical inadequacies of the political use of televisual communication. I have described the making of ideology through visual modes of presentation, because A New Beginning, perhaps more so than any other visual presentations to date, provides a vivid example of this process. It was by no means made apparent that the Republicans' symbolically constructed reality was an artifice designed to support their conservative ideology.

As Reagan's most comprehensive rhetorical display, the film exemplified the strategies and techniques that enabled the Republicans to communicate their version of reality to the American public, and in so doing, to achieve Reagan's enormous popularity and his landslide reelection victory in 1984. This study of their strategies has indicated many areas that require further investigation and analysis. Elaboration of televisual framing as it is used in future campaigns will help to demystify the ways that politicians use visual communication to convey authority and authenticity. The genre of the political campaign film needs to be investigated in depth in order to ascertain its relationship to A New Beginning. Another area of investigation concerns the relation of cultural myth and television. I have suggested that myths are often implicit and unarticulated; they are often re-presented in the forms of clichés that define a moral community. How do other televisual forms that express myths sustain or reinterpret ideology? I suggested some ways the "artful" presentation of visual clichés can serve an ideological function. Yet are they ever unsuccessful? Is their use ever trite, banal, and unpersuasive?

Finally, I considered the ways in which the film engaged the boundaries between fiction and reality in order to constitute an intelligible
reality. I left open the question as to what the inability to discern
shifting frames bodes for the future of America and Americans.

In this study I produced a reading of televisual film as a mode
of political discourse. *A New Beginning* was a product of a consumer
culture, a culture that consumes, most of all, images of itself, about
itself, which represent itself. Ronald Reagan was the consummate
image, able to unify and mask the contradictions that marked
American society and culture. He was a symbol that constituted and
was constituted by his "audience," the American people who accepted his fiction of discourse and his narrative authority.

Fortunately, a space still exists for criticism and analysis; such
metadiscourses can subvert the undemocratic impulses of this political usage of the media. Rhetorical criticism, in this case verbal discourse about visual discourse, can reframe and reconstitute a film as
part of an ongoing dialogue. Criticism is important as a tool to prevent subjection to discourse, to disrupt acceptance of a pseudospeech
on its own terms. *A New Beginning* did not reveal so much as it con-
cealed; it did not facilitate, but prevented questioning of reality; it
appropriated the means by which reality is conventionally constituted in order to re-present a familiar and reassuring version that was in
accord with conservative principles.

When political communication aims to cut off discourse, it is
not speech, it is pseudospeech, which compellingly frames, and is
framed by, an artificial "reality." Given television's centrality in
American culture, those with control of the media, (i.e., those with
resources), produce the images consumed by the television audience.
Those without resources, skills, or access remain unheard. As evidenced by Reagan's exclusion of undesirable members of society,
they cease to exist.

Further, both the Reagan administration policies and their
appropriation of televisual technology exemplified the widening
gaps between producers and consumers of social reality. It thus
becomes crucial for the viewing public, the "people" who are constructed by televisual discourses, to assume a different relation to the
televisual images and sounds that address them. Education is one
means of constructing this relationship, although social policies that
deemphasize education also serve to prevent critical viewer positions. Schools without funds can hardly afford personnel, materials,
or equipment in order to de-mystify visual communication forms;

making higher education the province of the few will also help keep the viewer in place, and will assure that television will not become an interactive and democratic medium. As it stands, television's transmission remains one-sided. Television, the modern cultural centerpiece, remains the communicative source and the viewers remain the consumers and receivers of messages. As such, viewers are supports for an exploitative ideology that feeds upon them in order to perpetuate itself.

Appendix

Text of *A New Beginning*

	Dialogue	*Image*
Scene 1		
	(Applause)	
JUSTICE: (OFF-CAMERA)	Governor, are you prepared to take the Constitutional oath?	Black screen with date, January 20, 1980, in white letters.
REAGAN: (OFF-CAMERA)	I am. *(Music)*	 Plow furrows earth as sun shines above.
	(Rooster Crows)	
JUSTICE: (OFF-CAMERA)	Place your left hand on the Bible and raise your right hand	Farmhouse in early morning sun, with truck moving out of frame.
	(Music)	
JUSTICE: (ON-CAMERA)	and repeat after me. I, Ronald Reagan, do solemnly swear	Documentary footage of Reagan inauguration
	(Music)	
REAGAN: (ON-CAMERA)	I, Ronald Reagan, do solemnly swear	
	(Music)	

JUSTICE: (OFF-CAMERA)	that I will faithfully execute the office of President of the United States.	Cowboy corrals horse; construction worker directs crane.
	(Music)	
REAGAN: (ON-CAMERA)	that I will faithfully execute the office of President of the United States.	Documentary footage of inauguration.
	(Music)	Boy on bicycle delivers papers in grassy suburb.
MAN: (ON-CAMERA)	Good morning, Jim.	Man carrying briefcase says hello to boy as he crosses sidewalk to waiting car.
	(Music)	
JUSTICE: (ON-CAMERA)	And will, to the best of my ability, preserve,	Documentary footage of inauguration.
(OFF-CAMERA)	protect, and defend	Traffic policeman guides construction workers across street
	(Music)	
REAGAN: (ON-CAMERA)	And will, to the best of my ability,	Documentary footage of inauguration
(OFF-CAMERA)	preserve, protect	Wooded camp area where flag is being hoisted.
	and defend	Children at camp gaze up at flag being hoisted.
JUSTICE: (OFF-CAMERA)	The Constitution	
	of the United States.	The Capitol building.
REAGAN:	The Constitution of	

(OFF-CAMERA)	the United States	
	(Music)	
JUSTICE: (ON-CAMERA)	So help you God. *(Music)*	Documentary footage of inauguration.
REAGAN: (ON-CAMERA)	So help me God. *(Music)*	
JUSTICE: (ON-CAMERA)	May I congratulate you, sir. *(Applause)*	

Scene 2

REAGAN: (OFF-CAMERA)	Yes, it was quite a day . . . a new beginning. You know, you don't really become president. The presidency is an institution, and you have temporary custody of it. I know that the image is that it's a lonely job, and uh, you're out there all on your own for everything that has to be decided or done. But that's not quite true. I've always believed that the other people around here are meant to be here and to contribute. And you know that the best council and the opinions and many times the varied opinions, opposition as	White House in early morning sun; close-up of Reagan at his desk; medium long shot of Reagan working alone at his desk; Reagan sitting at meeting; Reagan with Cabinet members; Reagan meeting with Tip O'Neill; Cabinet meeting.

well as approval of
what is being dis-
cussed. But, uh,
you're hearing these
honest views from
these very capable
men and women
who've given up so
much, so many of
them in their private
lives to come here and
serve, uh, you don't
feel alone. I believe
that the vice-presi-
dent, George Bush, is   Reagan walks with
more involved in poli-   Bush at White House.
cy matters of this
administration, gov-
ernment in general,
here in the executive
branch than any vice-
president we've

Scene 3

RONALD
REAGAN: probably ever had.   Medium close-up of
(OFF-CAMERA)   Bush seated in White
                                                House.

GEORGE BUSH: It's just different. The   Bush speaks in inter-
(ON-CAMERA)   mood is different.   view setting.
                        The, the . . . it's not
                        that everybody agrees
                        with what you're
                        doing, but there's a,
                        there's a certain
                        respect for the United
                        States of America and
                        it is loud, and it is
                        clear, and I, I run into
                        that all over the coun-

try. People say, "You know, we're pleased that the president is taking these strong positions, and they might, they might argue with you on one or two things if you give 'em a chance, but they're, back. You get the feeling that the country's moving again, a certain pride level.

Cut to Reagan reaction shot; back to Bush on-camera.

(Music)

Scene 4 *(On-Camera Interviews)*

MAN 1:

The bottom line with President Reagan is that he has brought back respect to the White House. Period, that's it.

Medium close-up of factory worker.

MAN 2:

There's a whole new attitude in America today. And I think that needs to be continued.

Medium close-up of black man in business suit, urban setting.

WOMAN 1:

It used to be the Americans took it for granted they were American. Now it seems like they're really proud.

Close-up of young woman with faint accent; pastoral setting.

MAN 3:

I feel more patriotic towards my country and I feel more proud to be an American.

Close-up of black worker on a construction site.

(Construction Noises)

MAN 4:	He put me to work, he's gonna keep me there. The man did a good job, and I hope he's gonna go for another four years. God bless America.	Close-up of construction worker wearing hard hat.
MAN 5:	I even hear songs on the radio, TV now that says I'm proud to be an American.	Close-up of elderly man, rural setting.

Scene 5

(Music)

SONG LYRICS:	If tomorrow all the things were gone I'd worked for all my life And I had to start again With just my children and my wife I'd thank my lucky stars To be living here today Cause the flag still stands for freedom And they can't take that away And I'm proud to be an American Where at least I know I'm free And I won't forget the men who died Who gave that right to me	Cityscape; yacht; waterfall; young child hugs her father; traditional wedding; house being built; family moves; welder at work; plow furrows the earth; close-up of flag; child salutes flag; Statue of Liberty under repair; two men in western garb converse; man at picnic smiles at camera; still photograph of Reagan at military funeral; policeman hoists flag; woman hugs soldier at picnic; still photograph of Americans waving flags; still photograph of Reagan surrounded by flag.

And I gladly stand up
  next to you
And defend her still
  today
Cause there ain't no
  doubt
I love this land
God bless the USA

Scene 6

REAGAN: (OFF-CAMERA)	Yes, there's been a lot of talk about a reawakened [sic] of patriotism in our country. And in our military, there's now a renewed sense of pride and patriotism there too. We recently were on a trip to Asia. On Sunday, in South Korea, I went up to the demilitarized zone, went to the outdoor church service with our troops there. *(Singing: Hymn)*	Air Force One; Korean army base; Reagan walking with soldiers; outdoor church service; Reagan singing hymns with troops.
CHAPLAIN:	May we bow our heads together for the invocation. *(Cafeteria Noise)*	Medium close-up of Reagan wearing army jacket.
REAGAN: (OFF-CAMERA)	I met with a great many of the men. I had the chance to talk with them individually, and I was so proud to hear not grumbling or I want to go home,	Reagan waits in line for a cafeteria lunch at the base.

	but to hear the pride with which they carry out their duties there.	
REAGAN: (ON-CAMERA)	It looks good.	Reagan takes tray from counter.
REAGAN: (OFF-CAMERA)	And I have never seen such morale, such esprit de corps, such pride in their work. All of us here at home should remember all those young men and women on the frontiers of freedom.	Long shot of cafeteria; medium shot of soldiers at tables; Reagan eating lunch with soldiers; soldiers stand in formation.
SOLDIER 1: (ON-CAMERA)	Steve (inaudible) from (inaudible).	Reagan shakes hands in barracks.
REAGAN: (OFF-CAMERA)	I hope that people out there recognize what a wonderful bunch of young people we've got in the military now. When they see someone on the street in uniform, I hope they'll go up and say hello and maybe tell them they're a little proud.	
REAGAN: (ON-CAMERA)	Proud to know you.	
SOLDIER 2: (ON-CAMERA)	Proud to know you too, sir.	

Scene 7 (On-Camera Interviews)

WOMAN 1:	The president's policies I'm 100 percent behind because he's	Close-up of middle-aged woman.

strong and he's strong defense.

WOMAN 2:	I think President Reagan is getting us back to basics, back to things that keep our nation surviving and strong, like a good defense and a good economy.	Close-up of middle aged woman
MAN 1:	The economy has never been as great as it has been now, uh, in twenty years, uh, unemployment is down, interest rates are down, uh, more people are buying homes than ever before.	Close-up of man wearing work clothes, urban setting.
MAN 2:	I really feel that we're gonna be better off in the long run.	Medium close-up of black man wearing suit, urban setting.
MAN 3:	We're on the upward swing. And the factories are working much stronger than before. The people are getting back to work.	Close-up of elderly man wearing golf hat, rural setting.
WOMAN 3:	People are traveling more, business is better, people on business trips, people on vacations—they're spending more money.	Close-up of young woman wearing business attire, urban setting.
MAN 3:	We're back on top.	Man 3 closes scene.

(Music)

Scene 8

REAGAN: (OFF-CAMERA)	You know it's hard to believe that it was less than four short years ago that interest rates were going through the roof. Inflation was, of course, the single biggest culprit and was responsible for those high interest rates. You can understand why tackling inflation head-on was one of our first priorities and we went at it tooth and nail and brought it down and we've kept it down.	Man welds; house under construction, close-up of nail being pounded; long shot of building frame; newspaper headlines read, "High Interest Rates," "Rocketing Inflation," "Inflation: Where Do We Go From Here," and "Here Comes the Recovery;" waitress takes order at diner; two men weigh fish; two workers give "thumbs up" sign; plow furrows earth.
REAGAN: (ON-CAMERA)	That wasn't wishful thinking. And it did become reality. Since January of '81 the prime rate has been pared by 40 percent. Mortgage interest rates have come down four percentage points since their peak. Now that makes home ownership possible for seven million American households that couldn't afford it just two and a half years ago. And	Medium close-up of Reagan sitting outside at White House.
(OFF-CAMERA)	the same goes for	Workers build house;

	automobiles too. Lower loan rates have made cars a lot more affordable for a lot more people. Still, it is good to see people buying homes and cars again, to see America's automobile industry regaining its strength and taking a back seat to no one. So	family moves into house with "SOLD" sign in front of it; child jumps into truck as her father stands in front of it and shakes hands with man in a business suit.
(ON-CAMERA)	we're going to keep on with what we're doing. We're going to bring those interest rates down further by keeping	Close-up of Reagan sitting outside at White House.
(OFF-CAMERA)	inflation down once and for all.	Newspaper headline reads, "A Break in Interest Rates."

Scene 9 (On-Camera Interviews)

WOMAN 1:	I think he's just dog-gone honest. It's remarkable. He's been on television, what have I heard, twenty six times? Talking to us about what he's doing? Now that's . . . he's not doing that for any other reason than to make it real clear. And if anybody has any question about where he's headed, it's their fault. Maybe	Close-up of woman in business attire, urban setting.

they don't have a tele-
vision.

(Music)

Scene 10

REAGAN: (OFF-CAMERA)	I've made a commit- ment, not just as pres- ident, but as a senior citizen myself that we must have a Social Security system that keeps its promise to the people who've kept their promise to America.	Elderly couple walk down suburban street; elderly couple in sil- houette walk along ocean.
(ON-CAMERA INTERVIEWS)		
MAN 1:	The president has done a lot of things, but bringing inflation down I think is proba- bly the best thing he's done for older people, for everybody.	Close-up of elderly man.
REAGAN: (OFF-CAMERA)	I feel strongly about keeping inflation down, interest rates down, but also mak- ing sure that no one pulls the rug out from under those people who are dependent on Social Security.	Elderly couple walk down street eating ice cream cones; elderly man hoists flag.
WOMAN 2:	I know that President Reagan is a caring man, that he cares about old people, and children, and ill people.	Close-up of elderly woman.

| REAGAN:
(ON-CAMERA) | There is no threat, from anyone, certainly not from this administration, to Social Security. | Extreme close-up of Reagan. |

Scene 11

(Crowd Noise-Voices Calling "President Reagan"

REAGAN: (OFF-CAMERA)	I didn't know I was shot. The—in fact I was still asking what was that noise. I thought it was firecrackers. And the next thing I knew Jerry, secret service, had simply grabbed me here and threw me into the car, and then he dived in on top of me. And it was only then that I felt a paralyzing pain and I learned that the bullet had hit me up here. When I walked in they were just concluding a meeting in the hospital of all the doctors associated with the hospital.	News footage of assassination attempt; newspaper headline, "Reagan Wounded, Outlook Good;" newspaper photographs of Reagan falling as he was shot; still photograph of Nancy Reagan visiting in hospital; still photograph of Reagan greeting assembly of hospital staff.
(ON-CAMERA)	Sure, when I saw all those doctors around me too, I said I hoped they were all Republicans.	Close-up of Reagan sitting outside at White House.
	(Laughter)	
(OFF-CAMERA)	I've been asked about	Still photograph of

	a visitor that I had while I was recuperating back in March of 1981, Cardinal Cooke. He was a wonderful man, a most dedicated man, and just one of the most kindly men that I have ever met.	Reagan meeting with Cardinal Cooke.
(ON-CAMERA)	And we were talking about some of the, call them coincidences that had happened at the time of the shooting and that I had heard after I'd started to recover. And he said that in view of them, God must have been sitting on my shoulder. Well, he must have been. I told him that whatever time I've got left, it now belongs to . . . someone else.	Close-up of Reagan sitting outside at White House.
	(Music)	

Scene 12

REAGAN: (OFF-CAMERA)	Our trip to Japan, Korea, and later the People's Republic of China makes you realize that the old line "Go West young man, go West" still fits. There's a new frontier out there, there's a future, and the United	Ocean; Japanese and American flags waving together; a crowd of Japanese waving American flags; Reagan waving to crowd of Japanese; Japanese children, Ronald and Nancy Reagan waving and

States is going to be very much a part of that future. One cannot meet with those people without realizing that they are a tremendously capable people, a talented and energetic people, and I found that there was a great longing for peace among those people. And I think that we can have a fine relationship, we do already. But we can keep that and build on that relationship, whether it's with trade, cultural exchange, we can be mutually beneficial to each other.

shaking hands with Japanese; close-up of hands being shaken; the Japanese palace; Reagan and group walking inside palace; horseman in archery display; Ronald and Nancy Reagan watch horseman from box and clap; the Great Wall of China; Ronald and Nancy Reagan walk along Great Wall with group of Chinese; Reagan shakes hands with Chinese premier.

Scene 13

REAGAN:
(OFF-CAMERA)

We stand on a lonely, windswept point on the northern shore of France. But forty years ago at this moment, the air was dense with smoke and the cries of men and the air was filled with the crack of rifle fire and the roar of cannon. Here in Normandy the rescue began at dawn on the morning of the sixth of June, 1944.

Ocean; cliffs at Normandy; Reagan gives speech to D-Day veterans, archival footage of: smoke-filled air, troops landing on beach at Normandy, battle scenes.

(Music)

REAGAN: (OFF-CAMERA)	Sixty two of the rangers who scaled the cliffs there at Pointe du Hoc, now back forty years later to the scene of their heroic action.	Long shot of Reagan giving speech to veterans; close-ups of veterans.

(Music)

REAGAN: (ON-CAMERA)	These are the boys of Pointe du Hoc. These are the men who took the cliffs.	Medium close-up of Reagan giving speech to veterans.
REAGAN: (OFF-CAMERA)	It was a very moving experience. They were what General Marshall called, "Our secret weapon—the best damn kids in the world." Where do we find them? Where do we find such men? And the answer came almost as quickly as I'd asked the question. Where we've always found them in this country—on the farms, in the shops, the stores and the offices. They just are the product of the freest society the world has ever known.	Close-ups of veterans as they listen to Reagan give speech; veterans stand and applaud Reagan; Reagan salutes; close-ups of flags and crosses which mark graves at cemetery; Ronald and Nancy Reagan walk through cemetery; close-up of Theodore Roosevelt's gravestone; Nancy Reagan lays flowers at Roosevelt's grave.

(Music)

REAGAN: (ON-CAMERA)	"Some day Liz, I'll go back," said Private	Medium close-up of Reagan giving speech

	First Class Peter Robert Zanatta, of the 37th Engineer Combat Battalion and first assault wave to hit Omaha Beach.	at podium.
(OFF-CAMERA)	Liza Zanatta Henn began her story by quoting her father, who promised that he would return to Normandy. She ended with a promise to her father who died eight years ago of cancer, "I'm going there, Dad. And I'll see the graves and I'll put flowers there just like you wanted to do. I'll feel all the things you made me feel through your stories and your eyes.	Close-up of Liza Zanatta Henn, medium close-up of Henn with family; long shot of ceremony; medium close-up of Reagan giving speech.
(ON-CAMERA)	I'll never forget what you went through, Dad. Nor will I let anyone else forget. And Dad, I'll always be proud."	Medium close-up of Reagan giving speech at podium.
(OFF-CAMERA)	Through the words of his loving daughter who is here with us today, a D-Day veteran has shown us the meaning of this day far better than any president can.	High angle shot of Liza Zanatta Henn as she sobs.
(ON-CAMERA)	It is enough for us to	Medium close-up of

say about Private Zanatta and all the men of honor and courage who fought beside him four decades ago, we will always be prepared so we may be always free. Thank you.

Reagan giving speech at podium.

(Music)

High angle shot as camera pans over treetops.

Scene 14

REAGAN:
(OFF-CAMERA)

I believe in the line "I look to the hills from whence cometh my strength." Before I reached my decision to run for re-election, some people thought that maybe I'd be happy to retire to that beautiful ranch outside Santa Barbara and spend the rest of my life enjoying the simple things, riding horses, chopping wood and spending time with Nancy, being outdoors and close to all of God's natural gifts. But they forget, there are so many things that remain to be done, so many challenges that must be met. I'd have felt like a quitter if I'd

Reagan rides his horse at his ranch; long shot of the ranch; a sign-post that reads, "The Reagan's;" Reagan grooms his horse; Reagan shoes his horse; Reagan saws wood; Reagan works on ranch with helpers; close-up of Reagan working in a T-shirt.

just walked away
from getting Federal
spending under con-
trol once and for all,
or from reforming and
simplifying our tax
system, creating enter-
prise zones, a set of
incentives that would
encourage business to
help rebuild the trou-
bled areas of our
country, provide hope
for those who yearn
for true opportunity.
And something
else . . .

Scene 15

REAGAN: (ON-CAMERA)	Sitting in the Oval Office, you look around and some-times you can't help but choke up a little bit because you're	Close-up of Reagan at his desk in Oval Office.
(OFF-CAMERA)	surrounded by history that somehow has touched everything in this room. And it occurs to you that every person who ever sat here yearned in the depths of his soul to bring people and nations together in peace.	Close-up of family photographs; pan of the Oval Office; close-up of a set of minia-ture soldiers from the Battle of Bastogne.
(ON-CAMERA)	Four times in my life America's been at war. That's a tragic	Close-up of Reagan at his desk in Oval Office.

waste of lives, and it makes you realize how desperately the world needs a lasting peace.

(OFF-CAMERA)   Just across the hall here in the White House is the Roosevelt Room, named after the two Roosevelts who served here, one a Republican, one a Democrat. Many decisions are made in that room, and often as I meet with my staff I gaze up at the five service flags, each representing one of the five military services. And draped from each flag are battle streamers, signifying every battle campaign fought since the Revolutionary War. Each ribbon a remembrance of a time when American men and women spilled their blood into the soil of distant lands.

Camera pans to Roosevelt Room, shot of service flags.

(ON-CAMERA)   My fondest hope for this presidency is that the people of America give us the continued opportunity to pursue a peace so strong and so lasting that we'd

Medium close-up of Reagan at his desk in Oval Office.

never again have to
add another streamer
to those flags.

(Music)

Scene 16

SONG LYRICS:

And I'm proud to be
an American
Where at least I know
I'm free
And I won't forget the
men who died
Who gave that right to
me
And I gladly stand up
Next to you and
defend her still
today
Cause there ain't no
doubt
I love this land
God bless the USA.

River runs between
mountains; cityscape;
policeman hoists flag;
a space shuttle lifts
off, veterans salute at
Normandy; flags and
crosses; still photo-
graph of Reagan with
the 1984 Olympic ath-
letes; construction
worker with his arms
folded across his
chest; still photograph
of young woman in
cornfield wearing
sign, "The USA, How
Sweet It Is;" Statue of
Liberty under repair;
Ronald Reagan and
George Bush walk
with their backs to the
camera; Ronald
Reagan with his arms
clasped over his head
in a victory sign.

Notes

Introduction

1. Diane Mermigas, "Nets Pressured on Reagan Film," *Advertising Age*, 23 August 1984: 53.

2. "CBS Rejects Reagan Film," *New York Times*, 24 August 1984: B5.

3. "Reagan Film Controversy the News at GOP Convention," *Broadcasting*, 27 August 1984: 35.

4. Richard Morgan and Dave Vadehra, "Reagan Leads Mondale in Ad Awareness Race," *Adweek*, 3 September 1984: 19.

5. Elisabeth Busmiller, "The Tuesday Team Wants America to Feel Good, *Adweek*, 29 October 1984: 70.

6. Steven R. Weisman, "The President and the Press: The Art of Controlled Access," *New York Times Magazine*, 14 October 1984: 71.

7. Mark Hertsgaard, "How Reagan Seduced Us," *Village Voice*, 18 September 1984: 12.

Chapter 1

1. Quoted by Peter Kaplan, "The Man Behind the Ferraro Ad," *New York Times*, 7 March 1985: C26.

2. See Kathleen Jamieson, *Packaging the Presidency: A History and Criticism of Presidential Campaign Advertising*. (New York: Oxford University Press, 1984), 43.

3. Jack Thomas, *Boston Globe*, 24 August 1984: 24.

4. Dudley Clendinen, "Actor as President: Half Hour

Commercial Wraps Him in Advertising's Best." *New York Times,* 14 September 1984: A18.

5. Jamieson, 94.

6. Before the ascendancy of television, political campaign films were shown in movie theaters. Calvin Coolidge's sixteen minute film biography, made in 1923, was one of the first political campaign films ever made. Harry Truman's 1948 biographical film was one of the most notable. It was assembled late in the campaign from existing footage. This strategy, born out of necessity, made the film seem indistinguishable from the newsreels people were accustomed to viewing, and the film was credited with playing a significant role in securing Truman's victory. See Jamieson, 32-4 for a more detailed description of this film.

7. Jamieson, 212-15.

Chapter 2

1. Erving Goffman, *Frame Analysis* (New York: Harper and Row, 1974), 10.

2. Gregory Bateson, *Steps to an Ecology of Mind* (New York: Chandler, 1972), 188.

3. Goffman, 22-23. Goffman's distinction between social and natural frames is paralleled by Sol Worth and Larry Gross's distinction between symbolic and natural sign events in *Studying Visual Communication* (New York: Mouton, 1980), 137, 141: If sign events are assessed as symbolic, implicative intent is assumed; that is, they are recognized to be persuasive. If they are read as natural, they are assumed to be informative and assessed on the basis of knowledge of the world in which they are found.

4. See Steven Neale, "Genre" in *Popular Television and Film,* ed. T. Bennett et al. (London: British Film Institute, 1981). Neale writes that in a number of fictional genres, discourses and codes overlap with those defined as nonfiction. He uses newspaper headlines as an example where "connotations of non-fiction spill over into or become attached to certain genres because some of their component discourses are also produced, classified, and circulated by institutions whose business is supposed to be 'facts' and 'truth' rather than 'fiction' or

'phantasy'" (20). Though Neale refers to the use of headlines in fiction films, the same holds true for their connotations of "nonfiction" in *A New Beginning*.

5. Bateson, 189.

6. Roger Silverstone, "The Right to Speak: On A Poetic for Television Documentary," *Media, Culture, Society* 5 (1983): 138.

7. John Ellis, *Visible Fictions* (London: Routledge and Kegan Paul, 1982), 128.

8. Daniel Dayan and Elihu Katz, "Electronic Ceremonies: Television Performs a Royal Wedding," in *On Signs*, ed. Marshall Blonsky (Baltimore: Johns Hopkins University Press, 1985), 27-28. Dayan and Katz elaborate upon the relationship between the narrator and the television event. Katz and Dayan also note (23-24) that television turns interactive ceremonies into spectacles. Though true interaction is destroyed, television simulates it anew by creating the impression of liveness and immediacy, as was the case with *A New Beginning*.

9. See Bill Nichols, "Voice of Documentary," *Film Quarterly* 36 (1983): 34-48. He also discusses the authoritative role of the narrator in *Ideology and the Image* (Bloomington: Indiana University Press, 1981), chapter 6.

10. Emile Benveniste, *Problems in General Linguistics* (Coral Gables: University of Miami Press), 1971.

11. Margaret Morse, "Talk Talk Talk: The Space of Discourse in Television" *Screen* 26 (1985): 2-17. Morse discusses discourse space as a virtual form of direct address in television, constituted by narrators who look directly out of the screen at viewers who are implied narratees. She argues that the resultant fiction of discourse offers a simulacrum of human sociality and exchange.

12. John Hartley, *Understanding News* (London: Methuen, 1982), 109-12. Hartley distinguishes between "institutional" and "accessed" voices. Institutionalized voices are fully "naturalized," and authoritative, so it seems that reality simply appears through them. Accessed voices are represented by interviews or reporters in the field. These voices are subordinate and less authoritative. The narration patterns of *A New Beginning*, while not specifically news, can be analyzed using Hartley's terms.

13. Rinker Buck, David Friend, and Christopher Wipple, "The Soft Sell, *Life* (June 1984): 80.

Chapter 3

1. Will Wright, *Sixguns and Society: A Structural Study of the Western* (Berkeley and Los Angeles: University of California Press, 1975), 176.

2. Ronald Reagan, Transcript of 1980 Inaugural Address. *New York Times*, 21 January 1981: A1.

3. James David Barber, *The Pulse of Politics: Electing Presidents in the Media Age* (New York: Norton, 1980), 210.

4. Kevin Phillips, *Post-Conservative America* (New York: Random House, 1982), 20.

5. Phillips, 20. Phillips names four areas that were in disarray prior to the Reagan presidency: economic, social and moral, nationalistic and patriotic, and institutional. Like many conservative theorists, he sees social and moral breakdowns as most responsible for political developments in the 1980s. From other perspectives, the 1980s were a reaction against liberalism's failure to fulfill its promise of equality. As the economic climate changed, inflation, limited resources, unemployment, and high taxes suggested to many that equality was a privilege reserved for times of abundance, not scarcity. See Zillah Eisenstein, "The Patriarchal Relations of the Reagan State," *Signs* 10 (1984): 329-37; and "The Sexual Politics of the New Right," in *Feminist Theory: A Critique of Ideology*, ed. Norman O. Keoshane, Michelle Z. Rosaldo, and Barbara Gelpi (Chicago: University of Chicago Press, 1982) 87-88.

6. See Gary Woodward, "Reagan as Roosevelt: The Elasticity of Pseudo-Populist Appeals," *Central States Speech Journal* 34 (1983): 44-45. Woodward states that American populism was a rural-based movement against the concentrations of wealth and power in the urban, eastern sections of the United States. The "people" were poor, virtuous, hard-working, and rural-based in small towns; they were opposed to corporate and governmental bureaucrats who were believed to be appropriating the wealth of "ordinary Americans." It is easy to see how Reagan continued this theme by opposing "the

people" to government bureaucrats and dropping corporate bureau-crats from the equation. See also Jeffrey Richards, "Frank Capra and the Cinema of Populism," in *Movies and Methods Volume I*, ed. Bill Nichols (Berkeley and Los Angeles: University of California Press, 1976): 65-77. Richards specifically relates American populism to films.

7. David Apter, "The New Mytho-Logics and the Specter of Superfluous Man," *Social Research* 52 (1985): 278, 287. Apter states "functional polarization represents a social tendency opposite to that emphasized in liberal theory, that is, the generalization of the middle sectors as a result of development." He argues that "the developmental tendencies which produced a generalized middle class, crucial to liberal notions of balance, mediation, and democracy, have begun to change to produce what might be called a polarization tendency.... It involves dispossession, displacement, and marginalization.... In turn, the latter can be defined as those who remove more from the social product than they contribute to it. Polarization, in this sense, is between the functionally significant . . . and the functionally superfluous, whose contributions to the rest of the society are negative (i.e., a tax on the rest of society)." Apter sees Western societies as increasingly representing this tendency, particularly the United States. Thus Reagan's construction of "the people," the generalized middle, glossed over the real contradictions at the foundation of American society. Accepting the Reagan image of American resurgence necessitated a simultaneous denial of the realities of postindustrial America.

8. Vincent Navarro, "The Industrialization of Fetishism and the Fetishism of Industrialization: A Critique of Ivan Illich," *Social Science and Medicine* 9 (1975): 357.

Chapter 4

1. See William H. Lewis, "Telling America's Story: Narrative Form and the Reagan Presidency," *Quarterly Journal of Speech* 73 (1987): 280-302. Lewis uses Walter Fisher's distinctions between rational and narrative paradigms to explain different responses to Reagan's rhetoric. Lewis's distinctions correspond to my notion of readers being "inside" or "outside" the myth. Those "inside" the myth accept it on the basis of its narrative logic, which is consistent

with their moral standards and commonsense understandings. Those "outside" the myth use a rational logic and evaluate Reagan's rhetoric on the basis of technical reasoning and substantive evidence.

2. Murray Edelman, *Political Language: Words that Succeed and Policies that Fail* (New York: Academic Press, 1977), 5.

3. See Walter Fisher, "A Motive View of Communication," *Quarterly Journal of Speech* 56 (1970). 131-39. Fisher names four basic rhetorical motives: affirmation, concerned with giving birth to an image; reaffirmation, concerned with revitalizing an image; purification, concerned with correcting an image; and subversion, concerned with undermining an image. He also suggests that rhetoric of reaffirmation produces a "real-fiction": "its subject matter and purpose refer to reality, but its advice cannot be empirically justified" (132). In a later article, "Rhetorical Fiction and the Presidency," *Quarterly Journal of Speech* 66 (1980): 119-26, he refers to real-fictions as rhetorical fictions and equates them with myth.

4. See Richard L. Johannesen, "Reagan's Economic Jeremiad," *Central States Speech Journal* 37 (1986): 79-89, and Paul D. Erickson, *Reagan Speaks: The Making of an American Myth* (New York: New York University Press, 1985) for applications of the jeremiad to Reagan's rhetoric. See also Karl Ritter, "American Political Rhetoric and the Jeremiad Tradition: Presidential Nomination Acceptance Addresses 1960-76," *Central States Speech Journal* 31 (1980): 153-71. Ritter examined acceptance addresses over a sixteen-year period and found they shared important characteristics with the jeremiad pattern. This chapter argues that *A New Beginning*, which immediately preceded Reagan's 1984 acceptance speech, was an even more powerful way to invoke the myth of rebirth; visual images that appeared to represent reality supplanted the verbal claims for America's "new beginning."

5. The first verse of Psalm 121 reads, "I will lift up mine eyes unto the hills, from whence cometh my help." Reagan says, "I look to the hills from whence cometh my strength," as he is riding his horse on his land in California. Reagan not only transposes "help" to "strength," but he changes what in the Bible is a paean to God to a literal tribute to life on his ranch.

6. James Hoban, Jr., "Rhetorical Rituals of Rebirth," *Quarterly Journal of Speech* 66 (1980): 276.

7. Hoban, 280-81.

8. See Walter Fisher, "Reaffirmation and Subversion of the American Dream," *Quarterly Journal of Speech* 59 (1973): 160-67. Fisher writes that the American Dream consists of two myths, materialism and moralism. When one version dominates, the other is subverted. American history may be interpreted as a constant struggle between reaffirmation and subversion of the materialist and moralist myths. Fisher recognized that the 1972 presidential election may have signaled a loss of faith in both versions of the American Dream. This loss of faith was later rectified by Ronald Reagan's rhetoric of reaffirmation, which revitalized both myths of the American Dream while it subverted the reality that contradicted the myths. However, some people—those operating from a rational model of critical judgment—remained unmoved by Ronald Reagan's myth of rebirth.

9. See Thomas Frentz and Janice Hocker Rushing, "The Rhetoric of Rocky: A Social Value Model of Criticism," *Western Journal of Speech Communication* 42 (1978): 63-72; 231-40. Frentz and Rushing explain how films can be vehicles that enact symbolic conflicts in order to shift value orientations.

10. Inflation was still at 9 percent at the time this film was shown. Similarly, although interest rates were down, they still remained higher than they had been in 1980.

11. Walter Fisher, "A Motive View of Communication," 132, 136. Fisher suggests that purification as a rhetorical motive is concerned with correcting an image. Reagan needed to redefine the past in a positive manner in order to unify Americans behind his strong defense policies.

12. See Kathleen Jamieson, *Electronic Eloquence in a Media Age* (New York: Oxford University Press, 1988), 162-64. Jamieson does an analysis of the D-Day speech, noting Reagan's ability to turn visual images into key themes of his presidency. See also Paul D. Erickson, *Reagan Speaks*, 38. Erickson remarks on Reagan's use of the line, "Where do we find such men . . . " in a 1972 speech, and notes that it was borrowed from a James Michener novel. Thus Reagan is quoting a line from his own 1972 speech in *A New Beginning*, a line that was itself drawn from fiction.

13. Reagan sits at his desk and holds a pen in his hand as he addresses the viewing audience. Upon close inspection, it is apparent that the pen is a Sharpie, a type of marker that is used to write on film, not paper.

14. Lou Cannon, *Reagan*, (New York: Putnam, 1982), 405.

15. Mark Hertsgaard, "How Reagan Seduced Us," *Village Voice*, 18 September 1984: 9.

Chapter 5

1. Thomas Frentz and Janice Hocker Rushing, "The Rhetoric of Rocky: A Social Value Model of Criticism," *Western Journal of Speech Communication* 41 (1978): 63-72, 231-240; and Janice Hocker Rushing, "The Rhetoric of the American Western Myth" *Communication Monographs* 50 (1983): 14-32. Frentz and Rushing write that American society consists of myths that exist in dialectical tension. Change occurs through dialectical transformation (an inversion from one prevailing set of values to another); synthesis (opposing sets of values become unified); emphasis (one oppositional element is stressed over the other); reaffirmation (the tension between opposites sets of values is restored); or pseudo-synthesis (opposing values are brought together effortlessly, masking their inherently contradictory nature. They assert that in the 1976 election, Carter enacted a dialectical synthesis, or integration, of materialistic and moralistic myths. Carter may have integrated opposing American myths during his election campaign, but his unsuccessful presidency furthered the subversion of American myths that had begun in the 1960s. In the latter article, Rushing argues that Reagan effected only a pseudo-synthesis of myths because he "created only the appearance of reconciling inherent opposites." However, Reagan did reaffirm both sides of opposing myths for those who chose to participate in his story. Only from a critical stance outside of the myth did he effect a dialectical pseudo-synthesis. From a critical stance, he appeared to reaffirm myths, but did so by eliding contradictions rather than reconciling or revitalizing opposing myths.

2. Robertson, 21-22. Robertson suggests that four basic questions structure American myths: what is the purpose of America; what is the place of the individual; what is the nature of community; and what is power for? Modifications of these questions are used here as myth of national purpose, place of the individual, the nature of community, and the appropriate use of power.

3. Walter R. Fisher, "Reaffirmation and Subversion of the

American Dream," *Quarterly Journal of SPeech* 59 (1973): 161-62. The summaries of materialist and moralist myths used here are taken from Fisher's article.

4. See Irving Kristol, "When Virtue Loses All Her Loveliness," in *Capitalism Today*, eds. Irving Kristol and Daniel Bell New York: Basic Books, 1971): 1-15; and Daniel Bell, *The Cultural Contradictions of Capitalism* (New York: Basic Books, 1976) for elaborations of this view from a neoconservative perspective.

5. See Will Wright, *Sixguns and Society: A Structural Study of the Western*, (Berkeley and Los Angeles: University of California Press, 1975), 137. Janice Hocker Rushing makes a similar point about the relationship between western heroes and social/historical/economic circumstances in "The Rhetoric of the Western Myth," 18-22; as does Sarah Russell Hankins in "Archetypal Alloy: Reagan's Rhetorical Image," *Central States Speech Journal* 34 (1983): 33-43.

6. Ronald H. Carpenter, "Frederick Jackson Turner and the Rhetorical Impact of the Frontier Thesis," *Quarterly Journal of Speech* 63 (1977): 123-24.

7. Carpenter, 124.

8. Robertson, 161.

9. See Sarah Russell Hankins, 41. Hankins writes that Reagan presented himself as a cowboy: "His image seems the political embodiment of the mythic Westerner." Walter Fisher, too, in "Romantic Democracy, Ronald Reagan, and Presidential Heroes, *Western Journal of Speech Communication* 46 (1982): 302 refers to Reagan as a "town marshall." Rushing, in "The Rhetoric of the American Western Myth," 26, also refers to Reagan's image as a cowboy, although she is aware of Reagan as a symbol of communalism. Reagan was as well known as a symbol of communalism as he was as a cowboy. In his film roles, he always played the average, ordinary American "nice-guy"; in his prepolitical career, he was the quintessential company man. He was well known as a spokesman for General Electric, delivering corporate messages to the American public. Thus, even while Reagan embodies the rugged individual, his image is also that of the cooperative, conforming member of society.

10. Robertson, 218-20.

11. Walter R. Fisher, "Rhetorical Fiction and the Presidency,"

Quarterly Journal of Speech 66 (1980): 119-20. Fisher argues that the presidency is a rhetorical fiction. This is "a generic term which encompasses in whole or in part persona, fantasy theme and rhetorical vision, political myth and ideology. . . . [E]ach of these concepts is a symbolic construction that exerts persuasive force in the making of persons, community, and the nation." Fisher asserts that ethos is the salient characteristic of the presidency as a rhetorical fiction, and that the key to this ethos is the president's conception of the people. In this sense, the people, as well as the presidency, are rhetorical fictions.

12. Fisher, "Romantic Democracy," 308.

13. Jeffrey Richards, "Frank Capra and the Cinema of Populism," in *Movies and Methods Volume I,* ed. Bill Nichols (Berkeley and Los Angeles: University of California Press, 1976), 68.

14. See Joseph Campbell, *The Hero With a Thousand Faces* (Princeton: Princeton University Press, 1968).

15. Wyckoff is quoted in Edwin Diamond and Stephen Bates, *The Spot: The Rise of Political Advertising on Television* (Cambridge: MIT Press, 1984), 102.

Chapter 6

1. Michael Osborn, "Rhetorical Depiction," in *Form, Genre, and the Study of Political Discourse,* ed. Herbert S. Simons and Aram Aghazarian (Columbia: University of South Carolina Press, 1986), 80-81. Osborn also notes that rhetorical depictions have five functions: presentation of experience, intensification of feeling, identification among those who participate in social communion, implementation of a plan of action, and reaffirmation of identity.

2. Anton C. Zijderveld, *On Clichés: The Supersedure of Meaning by Function in Modernity,* (London: Routledge and Kegan Paul, 1979), 10.

3. Joyce Nelson, *The Perfect Machine: Television in the Nuclear Age* (Toronto: Between the Lines, 1987), 69-70. Nelson cites Herbert E. Krugman, "Electroencephalographic Aspects of Low Involvement: Implications for the McLuhan Hypothesis" (New York: American Association for Public Opinion Research, 1970).

4. John Fiske and John Hartley, *Reading Television* (New York: Methuen, 1978), 117. Fiske and Hartley's notion of the oral logic of television is similar to what Kathleen Jamieson terms the associative grammar of television in *Electronic Eloquence in a Media Age* (New York: Oxford University Press, 1988): "Because television is a visual medium whose natural grammar is associative, a person adept at visualizing claims in dramatic capsules will be able to use television to short-circuit the audience's demand that those claims be dignified with evidence. . . . [P]art of Ronald Reagan's success is his ability to use visual vignettes to make unstated arguments" (13).

5. Bill Nichols, *Ideology and the Image* (Bloomington: Indiana University Press, 1981), 211. Nichols defines a poetic-image mosaic as follows: "The whole is not organized as a narrative but more poetically, as a mosaic; only the parts have a diegetic unity. Between sequences editing seldom establishes a chronological relationship; sequences follow each other consecutively but without a clearly marked temporal relationship. The whole thus tends toward poetry (metaphor, synchronicity, paradigmatic relations)—an all-at-once slice through an institutional matrix re-presented in time—rather than narrative" (211).

6. Nichols, 70.

7. Rinker Buck, David Friend, and Christopher Wipple, "The Soft Sell," *Life* (June 1984): 82.

8. See Judith Williamson, *Decoding Advertisements: Ideology and Meaning in Advertising* (London: Marion Boyars, 1983), 19. Though Williamson refers to advertisements, her point can be applied to *A New Beginning*, which was a hybrid documentary/advertisement.

9. Michael Osborn, "Archetypal Metaphor in Rhetoric: The Light-Dark Family," *Quarterly Journal of Speech* 53 (April 1967): 116-17.

10. George Lakoff and Mark Johnson, *Metaphors We Live By* (Chicago: University of Chicago Press, 1980), 14.

11. Christian Metz, *The Imaginary Signifier* (Bloomington, Indiana University Press, 1982), 46.

12. See John Hartley, *Understanding News* (London: Methuen, 1982). Hartley refers to people-on-the-street interviews as the "vox-pop." The term "refers to 'wo/man in the street' interviews which

are used to give flavour, reaction, or mood to issues that have been raised in the news. Hence their function is twofold. They authenticate the coverage given to particular events by showing the concern of ordinary people in the issue; and they serve as potential points of identification for the audience, who are presumed to share the style and 'widely held' opinions voiced in the vox-pop" (90).

13. See Nichols, 174-79. Nichols analyzes news and writes that witnesses (or interviewees) who give testimony serve as demonstrative proofs that authenticate the specifics of a given story and the authority of the program as a whole. The people-on-the-street who appeared in *A New Beginning* served this same function.

Chapter 7

1. See Hal Foster, ed. *The Anti-Aesthetic: Essays on Postmodern Culture* (Port Townsend, Wash.: Bay Press, 1983). For a more popularized explication of postmodernism, see Todd Gitlin, "The Postmodern Predicament," *Wilson Quarterly* 13 (1989): 67-76.

2. See Alvin Gouldner, *The Dialectic of Ideology and Technology* (New York: Oxford University Press, 1976), 168-70. Gouldner equates print media with rationality and electronic media with irrational, symbolic imagery. The position taken here is not that the electronic media are irrational, but that they manifest a different sort of rationality; that is, the oral, associative logic of television discourse as opposed to formal logic.

3. See Daniel Bell, *The Cultural Contradictions of Capitalism* (New York: Basic Books, 1976), 108.

4. Michael Osborn, "Rhetorical Depiction," in *Form, Genre, and the Study of Political Discourse*, ed. Herbert W. Simons and Aram A. Aghazarian (Columbia: University of South Carolina Press, 1986), 81.

5. Stuart Hall, "Encoding/Decoding," in *Culture, Media, Language*, ed. Stuart Hall et al. (London: Hutchinson, 1980), 136-38.

6. Walter Fisher, "Narration as Human Communication Paradigm: The Case of Public Moral Argument," *Communication Monographs* 51 (March 1984): 4, 8.

Chapter 8

1. Kenneth Burke, *The Philosophy of Literary Form* (New York: Vintage, 1957), 21.

2. Fredric Jameson, "Postmodernism, or the Cultural Logic of Late Capitalism," *New Left Review* 146 (1985): 58. Jameson names the following as constitutive features of the postmodern: (1) a new depthlessness, reflected in contemporary theory and the culture of the image; (2) a weakening of historicity, marked by the dominance of pastiche, nostalgia, and the breakdown of traditional categories; (3) the waning of affect; and (4) the "deep constitutive relationships of all this to a whole new technology, which is itself a figure for a whole new economic world system" (58).

3. Gregory Bateson, *Steps to an Ecology of Mind*, (New York: Ballantine Books, 1972), 188.

Selected Bibliography

Books and Articles

Andrew, Dudley. *Concepts in Film Theory.* Oxford: Oxford University Press, 1984.

Apter, David. "The New Mytho/logics and the Specter of Superfluous Man." *Social Research* 52 (1985): 269-307.

"Avalanche: The Reagan Mandate and How He Will Use It." *Newsweek* special issue Nov./Dec. 1984: ff.

Barber, James David. *The Presidential Character.* Englewood Cliffs, N.J.: Prentice-Hall, 1977.

———. *The Pulse of Politics: Electing Presidents in the Media Age.* New York: Norton, 1980.

Barthes, Roland. *Mythologies.* London: Grenada, 1980.

Bateson, Gregory. *Steps to an Ecology of Mind.* New York: Ballantine, 1972.

Baudrillard, Jean. *Simulations.* New York: Semiotext (e), 1983.

Bell, Daniel. *The Cultural Contradictions of Capitalism.* New York: Basic Books, 1976.

Benjamin, Walter. "The Work of Art in the Age of Mechanical Reproduction." In *Film Theory and Criticism,* ed. Gerald Mast and Marshall Cohen. 2d ed. New York: Oxford University Press, 1979, 848-70.

Bennett, Tony. "Media, Reality, Signification." In *Culture, Society, and the Media,* ed. Michael Gurevitch et al. New York: Methuen, 1982, 287-308.

———, S. Boyd Berman, C. Mercer, and J. Woolacott, eds. *Popular*

Television and Film. London: British Film Institute, 1981.

Bennett, W. Lance. "Myth, Ritual, and Political Control." *Journal of Communication* 30 (1980): 166-79.

———. "The Ritualistic and Pragmatic Bases of Political Campaign Discourse." *Quarterly Journal of Speech* 63 (1977): 219-38.

Benveniste, Emile. *Problems in General Linguistics.* Coral Gables: University of Miami Press, 1971.

Boorstin, Daniel J. *The Image: A Guide to Pseudo-Events in America.* New York: Harper and Row, 1964.

Bormann, Ernest. "A Fantasy Theme Analysis of the Television Coverage of the Hostage Release and the Reagan Inaugural." *Quarterly Journal of Speech* 68 (1982): 133-45.

———. "Fantasy and Rhetorical Vision: The Rhetorical Criticism of Social Reality." *Quarterly Journal of Speech* 58 (1972): 396-407.

Buck, Rinker, with David Friend, and Christopher Wipple. "The Soft Sell." *Life* (June 1984): 75-82.

Burke, Kenneth. *The Philosophy of Literary Form.* New York: Vintage, 1957.

———. *Rhetoric of Motives.* New York: George Braziller, 1955.

Burnham, Walter Dean. "The 1980 Earthquake: Alignment, Reaction, or Why." In *The Hidden Election*, ed. Thomas Ferguson and Joel Rogers. New York: Pantheon, 1981, 98-140.

Busmiller, Elisabeth. "The Tuesday Team Wants America to Feel Good." *Adweek*, 29 October 1984: 70ff.

Caesar, James W. "As Good as Their Words: Reagan's Rhetoric." *Public Opinion* June/July 1984: 10ff.

Campbell, Joseph. *The Hero With a Thousand Faces* (Princeton: Princeton University Press, 1968).

Cannon, Lou. *Reagan.* New York: Putnam, 1982.

Carpenter, Ronald H. "Frederick Jackson Turner and the Rhetorical Impact of the Frontier Thesis." *Quarterly Journal of Speech* 63 (1977): 117-29.

Caughie, John. *Imaginary Social Worlds.* Lincoln: University of

Nebraska Press, 1984.

"CBS Rejects Reagan Film, *New York Times*, 24 August 1984: B5.

Chaney, David. *Fictions and Ceremonies: Representations of Popular Experience*. New York: St. Martin's Press, 1979.

Clendinen, Dudley. "Actor as President: Half Hour Commercial Wraps Him in Advertising's Best." *New York Times*, 14 September 1984: A18.

————. "TV News: Effort to Balance Pictures with Words." *New York Times*, 3 October 1984: A24.

Collins, Richard. "Seeing is Believing: The Ideology of Naturalism." *Culture and Society* 5 (1983): 213-20.

Corcoran, Paul. *Political Language and Rhetoric*. Austin: University of Texas Press, 1979.

Curran, James. "Communications, Power, and Social Order." In *Culture, Society, and the Media*, ed. Michael Gurevitch et al. New York: Methuen, 1982, 266-81.

Dalleck, Ron. *Ronald Reagan: The Politics of Symbolism*. Cambridge: Harvard University Press, 1984.

Davidson, Osha. "The Rise of the Rural Ghetto." *Nation*, 14 June 1986: 820-22.

Davis, Howard, and Paul Walton, eds. *Language, Image, Media*. New York: St. Martin's Press, 1983.

Dayan, Daniel, and Elihu Katz. "Electronic Ceremonies: Television Performs a Royal Wedding." In *On Signs*, ed. Marshall Blonsky. Baltimore: Johns Hopkins University Press, 1985, 16-32.

Diamond, Edwin, and Stephen Bates. *The Spot: The Rise of Political Advertising on Television*. Cambridge: MIT Press, 1984.

Dougherty, Philip H. "Reagan's Emotional Campaign." *New York Times*, 8 November 1984: D20.

Edelman, Murray. *Constructing the Political Spectacle*. Chicago: University of Chicago Press, 1988.

————. *Political Language: Words That Succeed and Policies That Fail*. New York: Academic Press, 1977.

————. *The Symbolic Uses of Politics.* Chicago: University of Illinois Press, 1967.

Eisenstein, Zillah. "The Patriarchal Relations of the Reagan State." *Signs* 10 (1984): 329-337.

————. "Sexual Politics of the New Right." In *Feminist Theory: A Critique of Ideology,* ed. Norman O. Keoshane, Michelle Z. Rosaldo, and Barbara Gelpi. Chicago: University of Chicago Press, 1982, 77-98.

Ellis, John. *Visible Fictions.* London: Routledge and Kegan Paul, 1982.

Erickson, Paul D. *Reagan Speaks: The Making of an American Myth.* New York: New York University Press, 1985.

Evans, Rowland, and Robert Novak. *The Reagan Revolution.* New York: Dutton, 1981.

Ewen, Stuart. *Advertising and the Social Roots of Consumer Culture.* New York: McGraw Hill, 1976.

Farrell, Thomas B. "Political Conventions as Legitimation Ritual." *Communication Monographs* 45 (1978): 293-305.

Ferguson, Thomas, and Joel Rogers, eds. *The Hidden Election.* New York: Pantheon, 1981.

Fisher, Walter. "A Motive View of Communication," *Quarterly Journal of Speech* 56 (1970): 131-39.

————. "Narration as Human Communication Paradigm: The Case of Public Moral Argument," *Communication Monographs* 51 (1984): 1-22.

————. "Reaffirmation and Subversion of the American Dream." *Quarterly Journal of Speech* 59 (1973): 160-67.

————. "Rhetorical Fiction and the Presidency." *Quarterly Journal of Speech* 66 (1980): 119-26.

————. "Romantic Democracy, Ronald Reagan, and Presidential Heroes." *Western Journal of Speech Communication* 46 (1982): 299-310.

Fiske, John. *Television Culture.* New York: Methuen, 1987.

————, and Hartley, John. *Reading Television.* London, Methuen, 1978.

Foster, Hal, ed. *The Anti-Aesthetic: Essays on Postmodern Culture* (Port Townsend, Wash.: Bay Press, 1983).

Frentz, Thomas, and Janice Hocker Rushing. "The Rhetoric of Rocky: A Social Value Model of Criticism." *Western Journal of Speech Communication* 42 (1978): 63-72, 231-40.

Gelb, Lesley H. "The Mind of the President." *New York Times Magazine*, 6 October 1985: 20ff.

Germond, Jack, and Jules Witcover. *Wake Us When It's Over: Presidential Politics of 1984*. New York: Macmillan, 1985.

Gilder, George. *Wealth and Poverty*. New York: Basic Books, 1981.

Gitlin, Todd. "The Postmodern Predicament," *Wilson Quarterly* 13 (1989): 67-76.

Gledhill, Christine. "Klute 1: A contemporary film noir and feminist criticism." In *Women in Film Noir*, ed. E. Ann Kaplan. London: British Film Institute, 1978, 6-21.

Goffman, Erving. *Frame Analysis*. New York: Harper and Row, 1974.

Gouldner, Alvin W. *The Dialectic of Ideology and Technology*. New York: Oxford University Press, 1976.

Greenberg, Clement. "Avant Garde and Kitsch." In *Mass Culture*, eds. B. Rosenberg and D. White. Glencoe, Illinois: Free Press of Glencoe, 1962, 78-111.

Hall, Stuart. "Encoding/Decoding." In *Culture, Media, Language*, ed. Stuart Hall et al. London: Hutchinson: 1980, 128-38.

————. "Television and Culture." *Sight and Sound* 45 (August 1976): 246-52.

Hankins, Sarah Russell. "Archetypal Alloy: Reagan's Rhetorical Image." *Central States Speech Journal* 34 (1983): 33-43.

Hartley, John. *Understanding News*. London: Methuen, 1982.

Henry, William A. III. *Visions of America: How We Saw the 1984 Election*. New York: Atlantic Monthly, 1984.

Hertsgaard, Mark. "How Reagan Seduced Us." *Village Voice*, 18 September 1984: 1ff.

Hoban, James, Jr. "Rhetorical Rituals of Rebirth." *Quarterly Journal of Speech* 66 (1980): 275-88.

Hoberman, J. "Stars and Hype Forever." *Village Voice*, 29 January 1985: 11ff.

Huss, Roy, and Norman Silverstein. *The Film Experience: Elements of Motion Picture Art*. New York: Harper and Row, 1968.

Jameson, Fredric. "Postmodernism, or the Cultural Logic of Late Capitalism." *New Left Review* 146 (1985): 53-92.

Jamieson, Kathleen. *Eloquence in an Electronic Age*. New York: Oxford University Press, 1988.

————. *Packaging the Presidency: A History and Criticism of Presidential Campaign Advertising*. New York: Oxford University Press, 1984.

Jaroslovsky, Rich. "Manipulating the Media is a Specialty for the White House's Michael Deaver." *Wall Street Journal*, 5 January 1984: 48.

Johannesen, Richard L. "Reagan's Economic Jeremiad," *Central States Speech Journal* 37 (1986): 79-89.

Kaplan, Peter. "Film of Reagan for Convention Stirs TV Dispute." *New York Times*, 17 August 1984: A10.

————. "Introducing Reagan: Images and a Theme Song." *New York Times*, 21 August 1984: A19.

————. "The Man Behind the Ferraro Ad." *New York Times, 7 March 1985: C26*.

Kellner, Douglas. *"Network Television and American Society: Introduction to a Critical Theory of Television."* Theory and Society 10 (1981): 31-62.

Kelly, James. "Packaging the Presidency." *Time*, 12 November 1984: 36.

Kristol, Irving. *Two Cheers for Capitalism*. New York: New American Library, 1978.

————, and Daniel Bell, eds. *Capitalism Today*. New York: Basic Books, 1971.

Lakoff, George, and Mark Johnson. *Metaphors We Live By*. Chicago: University of Chicago Press, 1980.

Lewis, William H. "Telling America's Story: Narrative Form and the

Reagan Presidency," *Quarterly Journal of Speech* 73 (1987): 280-302.

MacDonald, Dwight. "A Theory of Mass Culture." In *Mass Culture*, eds. B. Rosenberg and D. White. Glencoe, Illinois: Free Press of Glencoe, 1962.

Maniaci, Tom (editor of *A New Beginning*). Personal Interview. 14 November 1985.

McArthur, Colin. *Television and History*. London: British Film Institute, 1978.

McLuhan, Marshall. *Understanding Media: The Extensions of Man*. London: Sphere Books, 1967.

Mellancamp, Patricia. "Situation and Simulation." *Screen* 26 (1985): 30-40.

Mermigas, Diane. "Nets Pressured on Reagan Film." *Advertising Age*, 23 August 1984: 1ff.

Metz, Christian. *The Imaginary Signifier*. Bloomington: Indiana University Press, 1982.

Morgan, Richard, and Dave Vadehra. "Reagan Leads Mondale in Ad Awareness Race." *Adweek*, 3 September 1984: 19.

Morse, Margaret. "Talk Talk Talk: The Space of Discourse in Television." *Screen* 26 (1985): 2-17.

Navarro, Vincent. "The Industrialization of Fetishism and the Fetishism of Industrialization: A Critique of Ivan Illich." *Social Science and Medicine* 9 (1975): 351-363.

Nelson, Joyce. *The Perfect Machine: Television in the Nuclear Age*. Toronto: Between the Lines, 1987.

Nichols, Bill. "Documentary Theory and Practice." *Screen* 17 (1976-77): 34-48.

————. *Ideology and the Image*. Bloomington: Indiana University Press, 1981.

————, ed. *Movies and Methods: An Anthology*. 2 vols. Berkeley and Los Angeles: University of California Press, 1976.

————. "Voice of Documentary." *Film Quarterly* 36 (1983): 34-48.

Nimmo, Dan, and James E. Combs. *Mediated Political Realities.* New York: Longman, 1983.

——— . *Subliminal Politics: Myths and Mythmakers in America.* Englewood Cliffs, N.J.: Prentice-Hall, 1980.

Osborn, Michael. "Archetypal Metaphor in Rhetoric: The Light-Dark Family," *Quarterly Journal of Speech* 53 (April 1967) 115-26.

——— . "Rhetorical Depiction." In *Form, Genre, and the Study of Political Discourse,* ed. Herbert S. Simons and Aram Aghazarian. Columbia: University of South Carolina Press, 1986, 79-100.

Phillips, Kevin. *Post-Conservative America.* New York: Random House, 1982.

Pollack, Norman, ed. *The Populist Mind.* New York: Bobbs Merrill, 1967.

Raines, Howell. "Reagan Sees Clear Choice." *New York Times,* 24 August 1984: A1ff.

"Reagan Film Controversy the News at GOP Convention." *Broadcasting* 27 August 1984: 35-40.

Reagan, Ronald. Transcript of 1980 Inaugural Address. *New York Times,* 21 January 1981: A1.

Ritter, Kurt W. "American Political Rhetoric and the Jeremiad Tradition: Presidential Nomination Acceptance Addresses, 1960-1976." *Central States Speech Journal* 31 (1980): 153-71.

Robertson, James Oliver. *American Myth, American Reality.* New York: Hill and Wang, 1980.

Rushing, Janice Hocker. "The Rhetoric of the American Western Myth." *Communication Monographs* 50 (1983): 14-32.

Schmid, Randolph E. "Concern Aired that Decline in Poverty Misses Minorities." *Oregonian,* 29 August 1985: A10.

Schwartz, Tony. *The Responsive Chord.* New York: Anchor, 1973.

Silverstone, Roger. "The Right to Speak: On a Poetic for Television Documentary." *Media, Culture, Society* 5 (1983): 137-54.

Smith, Hedrick. *The Power Game: How Washington Works.* New York: Ballantine, 1988.

Stiansen, Sarah. "Dusenberry Takes Film Fuss in Stride." *Advertising Age*, 27 August 1984: 64.

Stockman, David. *The Triumph of Politics*. New York: Harper and Row, 1986.

"Survey Finds that Big Companies Paying No Income Tax." *Oregonian*, 29 August 1985: F1.

Thomas, Jack. *Boston Globe*, 24 August 1984: 24.

Tudor, Henry. *Political Myth*. New York: Praegar, 1972.

Turner, Victor. *Dramas, Fields and Metaphors*. Ithaca: Cornell University Press, 1974.

Vestergaard, Torben, and Kim Schroder. *Language of Advertising*. Oxford: Blackwell, 1985.

Ward, Tom. "Sex and Drugs and Ronald Reagan." *Village Voice*, 29 January 1984: 14ff.

Weisman, Steven R. "Can the Magic Prevail?" *New York Times Magazine*, 29 April 1984: 39-55.

———. "The President and the Press: The Art of Controlled Access." *New York Times Magazine*, 14 October 1984: 35ff.

———. "Reaganomics." *New York Times Magazine*, 14 October 1982: 26ff.

"What Conservatives Think of Ronald Reagan: A Symposium." *Policy Review* 27 (Winter 1984): 12-19.

Williamson, Judith. *Decoding Advertisements: Ideology and Meaning in Advertising*. London: Marion Boyars, 1983.

Wilson, James Q. "Reagan and the Republican Revival." *Commentary* 70 (1980): 25-32.

Winniski, Jude. "The Mundell-Laffer Hypothesis—A New View of the World Economy." *Public Interest* 39 (Spring 1975): 31-52.

Wolfe, Alan. "Why the Neocons are Losing Out." *Nation*, 28 September 1985: 1ff.

Woodward, Gary. "Reagan as Roosevelt: The Elasticity of Pseudo-Populist Appeals." *Central States Speech Journal* 34 (1983): 44-58.

Worth, Sol, and Larry Gross. *Studying Visual Communication.* New York: Mouton, 1980.

Wright, Will. *Sixguns and Society: A Structural Study of the Western.* Berkeley and Los Angeles: University of California Press, 1975.

Zidjerveld, Anton C. *On Clichés: The Supersedure of Meaning By Function in Modernity.* London: Routledge and Kegan Paul, 1979.

Films and Television

A New Beginning. Prod. Phil Dusenberry. Republican National Committee, 1984.

Bush 1988 Political Campaign Documentary. Republican National Committee, 1988.

The Nixon Years: Change Without Chaos. 1972 Nixon political film.

The Democratic Faith: The Johnson Years. Democratic National Committee, 1968.

Dukakis 1988 Political Campaign Documentary. Democratic National Committee, 1988.

Ford 1976 Campaign Documentary. Committee to Re-Elect Ford, 1976.

Jimmy Who? Prod. Magus Corp. Philadelphia, PA, 1976.

The New Frontier. John F. Kennedy 1960 Campaign Documentary. Committee to Elect Kennedy, 1960.

Ronald Reagan 1980 Political Campaign Documentary. Republican National Committee, 1980.

Republican National Convention. ABC News Coverage. 23 August 1984.

Republican National Convention. CBS News Coverage. 23 August 1984.

Republican National Convention. NBC News Coverage. 23 August 1984.

This Man, This Office. Democratic National Committee, 1980.

Index

A

ABC news, 2
  convention commentary, 27
Abortion, 44
  See also Fundamentalists, New
    Right
Advertising, political, 2
  and commercial techniques, 4,
    16
  with documentary framing, 2, 9,
    10, 13, 15, 16, 20-24, 28-34, 72
Adweek
  media coverage vs. advertising
    survey, 3
Affirmative Action, 12, 44
Air Force One, 13, 70
American Dream, 35, 40, 44
  rebirth of, 57-68, 129
American Myth, American Reality,
  57
"A New Beginning" campaign
  film, 1, 2, 3
  and American myths or
    symbols, 6, 15, 22, 24, 27, 31,
    34, 41, 45-68, 69, 75
  analysis of, and methodology,
    93-100
  cost of, 1, 2, 4, 9
  and economic recovery themes,
    13-14, 15, 22, 58-61, 76
  and frame manipulation, 19-34,
    57, 69-82

and genre comparisons, 9-18,
    21-24, 28-34, 72, 98
  as news event, 9, 22
  and persuasion, 69-71, 97-100
  and "rebirth" implications, 15,
    15-16, 22, 23-24, 35, 40, 40-44,
    57-68, 75
  rhetoric as ideology in, 1, 3, 5, 6-
    7, 19-20, 22, 35, 40-44, 45-56,
    69-82
  script (dialogue and image),
    101-121
  See also Clichés, visual; Film(s),
    political campaign; Rhetoric
Audience. *See* Television, viewing
  audience

B

Bailey, Pearl, 13, 14
Barber, James, 39
Barthes, Roland, 46
Bates, Stephen, 4
Bateson, Gregory, 20, 24, 97
Baudrillard, Jean, 4
BBD&O advertising agency, 4
Benveniste, Emile, 28
Bicentennial celebration(s), 13
Boorstin, Daniel, 4
Brokaw, Tom, 26
Burke, Kenneth, 83, 93
Burnham, Walter Dean, 35
Bush, Barbara, 16